MW00597985

GOD'S COVENANT
with AMERICA

From Birth through the Nineteenth Century

BILL HUNTER

Illustration by Charles Timothy Prutzer

BROWN BOOKS PUBLISHING GROUP
DALLAS, TEXAS

GOD'S COVENANT WITH AMERICA
© 2004 by Bill Hunter
Printed and bound in the United States of America.

All rights reserved. No part of this publication may be reproduced, stored in any retrieval system, or transmitted in any form or by any means, mechanical, photocopying, recording, or otherwise, without permission in writing from the publisher, except by a reviewer, who may quote brief passages in a review to be printed in a magazine or newspaper.

All biblical quotes are either from the New International Version (NIV) or the King James Version (KJV).

For information, please contact:
Brown Books Publishing Group
16200 North Dallas Parkway, Suite 170
Dallas, Texas 75248
www.brownbooks.com
972-381-0009

ISBN 0-9741117-0-8
LCCN 2003107890
First Printing, 2004

Dedicated to America and the church. With their common vision, may mercy and truth meet together, and righteousness and peace kiss each other; may truth spring out of the earth; and righteousness look down from heaven.

—Psalm 85

CONTENTS

ACKNOWLEDGMENTS

Tim Prutzer is an outstanding artist, who seeks to paint from a Christian perspective. My wife, Jeanette, and I met him in the World Prayer Center in Colorado Springs where his portrait of a lion has been displayed. Specializing in wildlife, Tim carefully studies the biological history and details of his subjects. When asked if he would illustrate my book, he told me of a painting that he had appropriately named "Freedom," which he had worked on for over a year and a half. The painting on the cover of this book is a reproduction of that magnificent work. Tim says that the Native Americans called the depicted animal an eagle, but others call it a hawk. Tim's painting demonstrates the message of this book: America is a land of freedom, which has two natures. Like the eagle, it soars above and transcends all other nations' generosity, compassion, and expression of Christian values, but like a hawk, it devours its prey.

I have referred extensively to three books written by Peter Marshall and David Manuel, *The Light and the Glory, Sounding Forth the Trumpet,* and *From Sea to Shining Sea.* Through their exhaustive research, Marshall and Manuel presented the concept that has been forgotten by most Americans—that this nation was established with a covenantal relationship between God and our forefathers. These books are the best sources I have found that revisit this covenant in the period leading up to the Civil War and lay the foundation for the premise that this country is called to be one nation under God.

Through my friend, Stephen Lowrie, pastor of the First Baptist Church of Dalhart, Texas, I discovered J. Edwin Orr and his writings concerning revivals in America, from the revolutionary days through the first decade of the twentieth century. The great American revivals have sustained America's vision of a covenantal relationship with God. Because historians have primarily ignored the great revivals, most Americans have never heard of them, and since Orr's books are out of print, I have exhaustively described these great revivals using primarily Orr's writings.

Years ago, I read a book by Englishman Paul Johnson, entitled *The History of Christianity.* During my research, I discovered several more of his books, including *A History of the American People, Modern Times, A History of the Jews,* and *The Quest for God.* His writings have added historical continuity and integrity to this volume, as well as the upcoming second one.

Dr. J. Rufus Fears' series of teaching tapes, entitled "History of Freedom," were produced by The Teaching Company and were an invaluable source for my research. Dr. Fears has been an "outstanding professor" in various universities on many different occasions. Throughout these writings, I share ideas that I learned from Dr. Fears' "History of Freedom," and I express my appreciation for his willingness to read my manuscript and comment on it.

I appreciate the assistance of my publisher, Brown Books Publishing Group, and particularly Milli Brown, Kathryn Grant, and Alyson Alexander. Their assistance has been very professional, and this book is much better in every aspect because of their contributions.

Our friends, Bill and Debby Kruse, established a non-profit foundation, Rhema, to carry out their deep Christian commitment and to express their faith. Through Rhema, they and their other directors, Dean and Karen Eldridge and Kevin Eldridge, are generously financing this project. For their encouragement and financial support, I am deeply grateful.

I could not have accomplished this task without the assistance of my secretary, Toni Smith, and paralegal, Kathryn Lobley. Following my writings and dictations, Toni typed and retyped the chapters of this book, consistantly encouraging me to continue. Kathryn checked footnotes, provided suggestions, and performed many other essential services. Other members of my law office staff, Sandra Stenson and Michelle Aragon, also assisted in this project and provided support, for which I express my appreciation.

Most exciting to me has been the assistance of my family. My son, Michael Hunter, and daughter, Janet Tolbert, have tirelessly assisted in editing and redrafting this manuscript. My wife, Jeanette, has put up with three years of books all over the floor, has read and reread the manuscripts, and added valuable comments. Conversations with Jeanette, Michael, and Janet averted some narrow-minded perspectives of history that I might otherwise have taken. Our eldest daughter, Paula Butler, has taught me a great deal by demonstrating the American spirit that is so important for this nation. Through her professional career with family services in Utah, Paula works with abused children and is one of the most compassionate people I have ever known.

I thank you all.

INTRODUCTION

Let all the earth fear the Lord;
let all the people of the world revere him.
For he spoke, and it came to be; he
commanded, and it stood firm.
The Lord foils the plans of nations;
He thwarts the purposes of the peoples.
But the plans of the Lord stand firm forever,
the purposes of his heart through all generations.
Blessed is the nation whose God is the Lord,
the people he chose for his inheritance.

—Psalm 33:8–12 NIV

PARADOXICAL AMERICA

Amerca is different than other nations; it has drawn its citizens from all over the world. They came from every land and tribe and nation—often not knowing what they were looking for—but something drew them here. Often they came and then brought their families and friends because this nation gave them new hope and promise. Sometimes they were disillusioned and did not find what they had hoped for.

America is a paradox.
A refuge for the oppressed because it is a land of freedom.
A nation like a ship without a rudder that cannot determine what freedom means.
America is a paradox.
We are the most compassionate people in times of difficulty.
We are the most generous of all nations.
We remember the visions of our forefathers; we proclaim their dreams in our assemblies.

This is what draws others to America; it is that nature which has brought people from all over the world, from every land and tribe and nation to be a part of this land of freedom. But there is another side of America.

We are the most self-serving of all people.
We are a lawless and rebellious people.
Our idea of freedom is to be left alone to do what we want to do; we want to make our own rules.
We are obsessed with sex and violence; we exploit it in movies, television, and videos throughout the world.
We have sacrificed millions of children in their mothers' wombs.

We have experienced God's blessings, and we have seen God's curses. We have witnessed God's divine intervention to preserve and protect our nation. At the same time, we have seen God's judgment through national disasters, a high crime rate, a high divorce rate, a high incidence of neglected children, and poverty that is beyond belief in a nation of such prosperity.

Our forefathers and our national leaders have referred to America as a Christian nation; but like a wayward child, we have turned away from our fathers' visions. However, there is something within us that will never permit us to get away from our fathers' dreams. Something within us reminds us of the call that God has on this nation; there is a striving within us for more; we cannot get away from the influence of our fathers. Ultimately, our forefathers' vision will define our lives, or we will spend all of our days running from it.

I have written two volumes which describe America's history from its birth to the present, *God's Covenant with America.* The subtitle of this volume is *From Birth through the Nineteenth Century.* The subtitle of the second book is *The Dawn of a New Day.*

In researching this nation's history from a Christian perspective, I have concluded that there are four primary periods of God's intervention in the history of America:

(1) Our forefathers came to America seeking religious freedom and dedicated this nation to God. When God accepted that dedication, a covenant was established. The covenant "of the people, by the people and for the people," was established by our Declaration of Independence and our Constitution, which are two of history's greatest documents and inspired by God to survive the ages. The first part of this book presents the story of our forefathers' arrival in America, their struggles to survive, and God's intervention on their behalf, which led to the formation of a new nation and the drafting of the

Constitution. Since readers of this book have access to comprehensive historical accounts of America's revolutionary days and early national heritage, the chapters of this first part present a brief overview of America's early history. The primary task of these first chapters is to present a picture of God's divine intervention in the formation of this land of promise.

(2) Part Two, which covers the nineteenth century, focuses on the events that have defined this nation, which I refer to as "The Essence of Freedom." During the first sixty years of the nineteenth century, there were two great spiritual revivals (sometimes called "three awakenings") that shaped the conscience of America and prepared it for the Civil War. It is my premise that, for good or bad, the seeds of America's interpretation of liberty and freedom were planted in the nineteenth century. During the nineteenth century, the two great struggles were over slavery and states' rights, which led this nation to its great Civil War. During the Civil War, Abraham Lincoln believed that the United States could survive even in the midst of divisive circumstances. When Robert E. Lee realized that the South could not prevail, he cast his lot to do everything possible to bring unity in the midst of division. This second part describes in more detail the events that shaped the destiny of America.

(3) The second book begins with the twentieth century revival that started in Wales. Most Americans have never heard of this great worldwide revival that took place in the first decade of the twentieth century and prepared this nation for the tremendous struggles of two world wars, a great depression, and the Holocaust. Out of such darkness and despair, God's plan unfolded for the formation of the nation of Israel as the first land of promise and the determination of the destiny of

America as the second land of promise. This God-ordained plan began to unfold in the last half of the twentieth century. During the last fifty years, a great struggle occurred between two forces: a) those who would seek to preserve America's concept of freedom based on the equality of all men (liberty) and absolute principles of right and wrong (truth); and b) those who believe that freedom means the right to do what one chooses without any restraint. "To the victors belong the spoils," and the winner of this struggle will determine whether this nation will move toward its call as one nation under God or toward anarchy.

(4) At the end of the second book, look through a glass dimly for a vision of God's plans for America in the new millennium. There is great anticipation in the Church and in American secular society that dramatic things are about to happen in America. There are many in the Church who anticipate a move of God that is greater than anything that has ever happened in this nation, and there are clear signs that a great worldwide revival is now beginning.

The one expression that has been used the most to distinguish America is the phrase "land of freedom." Therefore, I must furnish some explanation of that term before I write of this nation's history. Even though freedom is our greatest attribute, we struggle to define that term, and every American has his own definition. To define this term is difficult because we have swept away every premise of true freedom upon which this nation was founded, and herein lies America's greatest crisis of identity. As a national expression, there can be no definition of freedom except based on underlying truths; then those truths provide the definition of freedom. When one says, "I am free," it is always appropriate to ask, "Free to do what?" The statement of Jesus, "You shall know the truth, and the truth shall set you free," is one of the most profound statements concerning our relationship with God and others. Freedom must be based on underlying truths, and the best expression of those truths that motivated our forefathers to come to this new land is found in the Word of God.

Jesus summarized the Word of God (truth) with one statement: "Love the Lord your God with all your heart and with all your soul and with all your mind. This is the first and greatest commandment. And the second is like it: Love your neighbor as yourself. All the Law and the Prophets hang on these two commandments." (Matthew 22:37–40 NIV)

To the extent that a group of people seek to love, respect, and care for each other and follow God's mandate to do what is right and refrain from what is wrong, they will live in liberty and freedom; then there will be a definition of freedom—to be free to share their common bond of love.

The book of Judges ends with one of the most disturbing statements: "In those days there was no king in Israel; every man did what was right in his own eyes." (Judges 21:23 KJV)

This is also a profound statement epitomizing America's recent history. Our nation has swept aside every vestige of truth by removing God from our schools and public forums; in the process we have substituted "situation ethics" as our behavioral guideline. One of America's most highly respected Supreme Court justices, Oliver Wendell Holmes, Jr. (1841–1935), was quoted as saying that "Truth is the majority vote of that nation that could lick all others."[1] Justice Holmes also categorically dismissed truth as a foundational principle of law: "So when it comes to the development of a corpus juris the ultimate question is what do the dominant forces of the community want and do they want it hard enough to disregard whatever inhibitions may stand in the way."[2]

Chief Justice Frederick Moore Vinson (1890–1953) stated that "nothing is more certain in modern society than the principle that there are no absolutes."[3]

If ethics—which change with every situation—are our guidelines, *there can be no definition of freedom as a national expression.* Then our leaders may redefine freedom with each change of the national scene. This is what has happened in America. It was evident in America's history during the eighteenth and nineteenth centuries:

When the South needed cheap labor to sustain its tobacco industry, slavery was introduced.
When America found rich and fertile land occupied by Indians, the Indians were displaced.
When America sensed a divine mandate to expand from the Atlantic Ocean to the Pacific Ocean, it started the Mexican War.
When the North and the South struggled over states' rights and the rights of slaves and competed over control of the United States Congress, the great war between brothers occurred.

Application of principles of freedom without greater underlying foundational truths will *inevitably* result in injustice. The operative word is "inevitable," for freedom that is not founded upon greater underlying principles will inevitably lead to oppression; it will always favor one group over another and produce inequity. Without love, without true compassion, leaders will *inevitably* manipulate one group in order to promote another.

Many nations were founded on expressions of the grand idea of freedom; many leaders have proclaimed it; many people have blindly followed believing that their leaders were leading them to a time of freedom only to see that the end of their pursuit was oppression. In the name of freedom there have been many examples of oppression. Freedom has been expressed by those who demand that their citizens accept the ideology of the leaders (such as the church-states of Europe) or by persecution or servitude of groups in order to foster freedom on behalf of others (such as America's treatment of the Native American Indians and the blacks in the eighteenth and nineteenth centuries).

As America drifted from its Christian heritage, national and religious leaders observed the nation's moral decline and have sought to force their own ideological demands on the citizens. Some of the loudest voices proclaiming that the people of this nation must conform to their standards have been the leaders of the Church, often with a self-righteous and arrogant attitude. It is one thing for Christian leaders to exhibit the nature of Christ and by their example encourage others to follow; it is quite another to judge the conduct of Christians and non-Christians by a standard that is not evident in the lives of the standard bearers. America has seen too many highly visible examples of the latter.

The non-Christian society and many Christians in America have been offended by efforts of Christian leaders to dictate American morality and primarily by the self-righteous attitude of many of America's Christian leaders. This has produced a counter-reaction in American society, which is seen in three major thrusts:

(1) A large part of America's society, particularly intellectuals and youth, have rejected Christianity, and with it, Christian principles. Instead of absolutes, they have accepted "situation ethics" and have determined that every man does what is right in his own eyes. *Situation ethics* is the logical expression of freedom in a society devoid of moral restraint. There is a large segment of American society that proclaims one way or another, "I want to be free to do what I want to do when I want to do it. I want to make my own rules." This has produced

a pleasure-seeking attitude and a desire to be left alone that pervades American society, including the churches.

(2) America has become a nation of many gods. Since many Americans do not believe the Christian church is relevant and do not accept Christianity, they have sought other spiritual and philosophical expressions; many religions have emerged in America that include New Age religions and satanic religions such as voodoo, witchcraft, and Wicca.

One of the most amazing developments in America's history in the twentieth century has been the systematic rejection of truth. This is evident in the decisions of the Supreme Court; it is expressed in our schools and public forums; it is even expressed in our churches. In an amazing turn of events, this nation, founded by our forefathers as one nation under God, has elevated humanism to a more acceptable religion than Christianity. In the last part of the twentieth century, tolerance was considered fashionable, and any expression of truth was considered narrow-minded, bigoted, and prejudicial. In early days in America's history, one could proclaim God's Word to the nation and the blessings of obedience and the judgments of disobedience. By the twentieth century, such proclamations were unacceptable. The loudest voices were raised against Christian leaders who sought to express Christian values to the nation.

(3) America's history of oppression of races and classes has produced a rage among minority groups and underprivileged citizens that has made our inner cities a battleground. This same attitude of rage has extended to public schools and colleges and pervaded television, videos, and movies so as to become a national expression of rebellion, lawlessness, and immorality. College students and intellectuals are often outraged by the

injustices and oppression that the American imperialistic society has produced and the shallow, meaningless statements of leaders in defense of this American way.

The contradictory position of America's proponents of freedom is evident. On one hand, those who fear that individual rights of citizens will lead to anarchy are quick to defend their own rights to do what they choose. On the other hand, those who take a strong stand in defense of their own individual rights demand that the government intervene to protect their exercise of freedom even though that exercise of freedom infringes upon the rights of others. It is most evident in the abortion issue. Women who insist on the right to do what they choose with their own bodies are willing to eliminate a class of people (the unborn children) in order to foster their own interests.

In the last few years, the study of America's Christian history has consumed me. The hope and promise that this nation will fulfill its destiny as one nation under God has driven me. It has led me to cry out to God that America will not miss its calling.

It has planted a desire that I will live long enough to be a part of that great revival which I believe will occur throughout the world starting in America, centered in one man, the Man Christ Jesus.

These writings will reveal the cry of my heart for America. Hopefully, they will, at least in part, reveal the heart of God for this nation.

Part 1

FREEDOM

Nothing is so powerful as an idea whose time has come.

—Victor Hugo, nineteenth-century French author
whose writings include *Les Misérables*

"Woe to me," I cried. "I am ruined! For I am a man of unclean lips, and I live among a people of unclean lips, and my eyes have seen the King, the Lord Almighty."

Then one of the seraphs flew to me with a live coal in his hand, which he had taken with tongs from the altar. With it he touched my mouth and said, "See, this has touched your lips: your guilt is taken away and your sin atoned for."

Then I heard the voice of the Lord saying, 'Whom shall I send? And who will go for us?' And I said, 'Here am I. Send me!' He said, 'Go and tell this people.'"

—Isaiah 6:5–9 NIV

THE CALL

On a day in the late twentieth century in Williamsburg, Virginia, a man sat in a convention center watching a movie of the noble action of the founders of this nation as they prepared to fight for their independence. While the man watched, tears ran down his cheeks. Realizing it was the move of God on his life, the man lifted his eyes to Heaven and said, "Father, what are you doing?" The Father spoke to him and said, "I am leading you into a commitment to this nation that is beyond anything you could imagine."

Years passed and times changed and many times the Father spoke to this man, but always those words of the Father rang in the man's heart. At first the man envisioned glorious manifestations of the Father's words, although he saw no evidence of them and could not imagine how they could happen. Finally, the Father focused the man's attention on one word that the man had never noticed. That word was "commitment"— a word the man did not want to hear. Finally, the man's heart began to change as he focused on the word "commitment," and then the Father spoke to him again:

"My son, you are my friend. I have watched you and prepared you. My Spirit has led you and trained you and fixed your eyes on my Son. You have learned to live in my Son and to strive to glorify Him by your life, but the words you have never wanted to hear are 'commitment' and 'obedience.' You have a passion for this country and for your city, and a desire to see your city transformed and this nation established as one nation under God. But your passion is without vision. It is without zeal or commitment.

"I will plant in you my vision of this nation. The vision I plant in your life will be flawed from the beginning because it will include your thoughts, your studies, and your preconceptions. But my vision will

be planted by my Spirit. As time passes, as you listen to my Spirit and seek to understand my ways and ponder the words 'obedience' and 'commitment,' the clarity of my vision will unfold.

"In time, the covenant I made with the founders of this country as 'one nation under God' will be planted in your spirit with a clarity that you cannot now comprehend. Then you will know what I meant when I told you I will lead you into a commitment to this nation beyond anything you can now imagine.

"At times you will back away because it is inconceivable that I could plant such a glorious word in such an ordinary man, but remember my ways are always revealed through imperfect vessels."

And now the man's journey begins—a journey founded on a passion that his city will be transformed and his nation will be one nation under God. The cry of his heart is, "Father, show me your vision for my city and my nation. Plant that vision in my heart. Teach me the meaning of the words 'commitment' and 'obedience.' Set my face like flint to serve you and to see this nation unfold as 'one nation under God.'"

Chapter 1

The chariots of God are tens of thousands and thousands of thousands;

the Lord has come from Sinai into his sanctuary. When you ascended

on high, you led captives in your train; you received gifts from men,

even from the rebellious—that you, O Lord God, might dwell there.
                              —Psalm 68:17–18 NIV

Not like the brazen giant of Greek fame,
With conquering limbs astride from land to land;
Here at our sea-washed, sunset gates shall stand
A mighty woman with a torch, whose flame
Is the imprisoned lightening, and her name
Mother of Exiles. From her beacon-hand
lows world-wide welcome; her mild eyes command
The air-bridged harbor that twin cities frame.
"Keep, ancient lands, your stored pomp!" cries she
With silent lips. "Give me your tired, your poor,
Your huddled masses yearning to breathe free,
The wretched refuse of your teeming shore.
Send these, the homeless, tempest-tost to me.
I lift my lamp beside the golden door!"
                    —Inscription, Statue of Liberty
                  (Emma Lazarus, "The New Colossus")

THE GATHERING

*T*he Comforter planted in the heart of the man a vision of America's most important asset—its people. In a panoramic vision, the man saw how they came. There were those who were here at the beginning—the ones called Native American Indians or simply Indians. They possessed and loved this land before the others came. They knew the land like no other would ever know it. They were born with an acute comprehension of both the natural and the divine. Although they lived an ocean away from the place of the cross and had never heard of the Crucified One, there was something within them that planted a revelation of the Father. They saw it in the rocks and trees; they saw it in the stars; they heard it in the wind; all of nature revealed it to them: a constant revelation of the divine.

The man tried to imagine what would have happened had their natural comprehension of the divine been joined with a revelation of the Crucified One when the Christians came to America from Europe. And yet, when the Europeans came, they drove these Indians from their own land and treated them as savages and infidels.

There were those who came in early days, by boat and by land, across the rugged north land that we know as Iceland, Greenland, Labrador, and Canada on the east, and Russia, Alaska, and Canada on the west. Most of them settled in Canada and the northern territories of the United States. They planted a fierce spirit of independence and self-determination that grew out of their struggle with the land.

The man agonized over those who came from Africa, who came not of their own choosing. They were torn from their homes and cast into boats like animals and shipped from Africa to America to be slaves of the affluent and servants of the land. Many of these African Americans died on the journey, and those who survived not only served as slaves, but were treated in the vilest, most humiliating ways.

Yet these African Americans, through their personal relationships with the Father, the Son, and the Holy Spirit in times of suffering, planted a vision of the suffering Christ. The treatment they received at the hands of their fellow Americans was to create a paradox in this land—a curse and a blessing—a curse because of the hate and division between races that developed, and a blessing because of their sacrificial courage borne out of their faith in God in their days of suffering.

But most of the early Americans came from Europe across the great ocean. They first came in small numbers like the trickle of a small stream, then like a larger stream, and finally, like a mighty river. The man pictured their coming. As the first ones came, they traveled in ships that were not prepared for the mighty ocean. Many died on their journey. The early travelers who survived were not prepared for the rugged land and harsh winters. Many of those who survived the trip across the ocean died in their first year in America; but the difficult journey, rugged land, and harsh winters would not keep others from coming.

There were those who came for religious freedom who settled in the northeast along the Atlantic coast. Others settled in Virginia and the other natural east coast ports. Many came for adventure and for fortune. When they arrived, these new Americans sent letters to their friends and relatives in their motherland which contained, in one form or another, this message: "Come—this is the land of promise—this is it." And others came in response to their calling. The newcomers settled everywhere in the new land, practicing trades they had learned in their motherlands or new trades that they adopted for survival.

The man pictured Ellis Island and the mighty Statue of Liberty, with its torch of freedom and famous inscription welcoming the immigrants. Millions and tens of millions came from all over the world, from every nation, from every race, from every culture, from every religious background—and the only thing that kept others from coming were the American laws that limited immigration.

The first great development of the nation was in the Northeast. Because of the rough winters there, this was the greatest point of challenge in the new land. But it soon became the most populous area, revealing the indomitable spirit of our forefathers. The new settlers met each challenge that this rugged territory had to offer. When they conquered one area, they moved to the next, which often was even greater, until our pioneering forefathers had settled in all of the wild, rugged land of America. Although it appeared to take a long time, when compared with the history of other nations, the settlement of our forefathers in all of the land of promise was only as a moment.

Although the first great river of new Americans came from Europe, seeking religious freedom and a new life, there were others who came from the South, which included many islands, Mexico, and South America. During the early colonial days, Texas, New Mexico, Arizona, and California were a part of the Spanish territory, and then later a part of the Mexican territory.

Through the influence of Spain and Mexico, Roman Catholic missions were planted throughout the newly settled territory of the Southwest. Those who came from South America and the many islands to the south brought with them the influence of the Roman Catholic Church; but many of those who came also planted strongholds of voodoo, witchcraft, and black magic in the southern cities of America. Later, rivers of immigrants came from Asia, North Africa, and other countries, bringing with them their customs and religions until, in this day, all nations of the world and all religions are represented in this new land of promise.

The man pondered all of these events and lifted his eyes to the Father with one big question: "Why have you brought people of all reli-

gious backgrounds, of all nations, of all races to this land? Nothing like this has ever happened in any place on earth. What are you doing here?"

And the Father answered, "You call some of your cities melting pots because people have come from all over the world into your cities. It is my intention that this nation will be a great melting pot of all people, of all races, of all religions, over which my Son shall be acknowledged as Lord. Remember that I brought them here for a purpose. Your journey will be to discover the vision and plans I have for them. I will lead you on a journey through the history of the United States so that you may see—through a glass dimly—my plans for this nation and the glory of my Son."

Chapter 2

We feel, due to the extreme gravity of America's present
spiritual and moral condition, that it is imperative that we Americans
rediscover our spiritual moorings.

Once it had become clear that God did have a plan for
America, our search for evidence of this plan became akin to
tracking a rich vein of gold through a mountain. The vein
of gold had three main characteristics, as follows:

*First, God had put a specific 'call' on this country and
the people who were to inhabit it.*

*Second, this call was to be worked out in terms
of the settlers' covenant with God, and with each other.*

*God did keep His end of the bargain (which is the
third major theme), and He did so on both an
individual and a corporate basis.*

In fact, there seemed to be a continuing, almost predictable
cycle: in great need and humility a small body of Christians would
put themselves into the hands of their Lord and commit their lives to
one another . . . But as they grew affluent, they would also become
proud or complacent or self-righteous.

Nonetheless, the blessing would continue unabated, sometimes for generations, as God continued to honor the obedience of
their fathers and grandfathers. See Deuteronomy 7:9.

Yet in the early days of our history, it is astonishing to see how few people it took to begin a cycle of repentance, followed by the return of God's grace. *And so, this was the final major theme we found: that when a group of people, no matter how small or ordinary, was willing to die out to their selfish desires, the life which came out of that death was immeasurable, and continued to affect lives far into the future."*

—from the 1977 book *The Light and the Glory,*

by Peter J. Marshall, Jr., and David B. Manuel, Jr.

(italics added)

GOD'S PLAN FOR AMERICA

Starting in the 1970s, Peter Marshall and David Manuel co-authored three books: (1) *The Light and the Glory*, which describes the formative days of this nation; (2) *From Sea to Shining Sea*, covering the history of America from 1787 to 1837, which was this nation's great expansion period; and (3) *Sounding Forth the Trumpet*, which covered the events leading to the Civil War.

In the 1970s, when *The Light and the Glory* was written, America had forgotten its godly heritage. During the last half of the twentieth century, schools throughout America have denied the Christian vision of Columbus, Washington, and Lincoln, along with the other great leaders that led America in the formative periods of its history. Peter Marshall was the son of the late renowned Senate chaplain of the same name, and Catherine Marshall, best-selling Christian author. Despite his Christian and political heritage, Peter Marshall was surprised to see the extensive intervention of God in the defining events of our nation. These three books of Marshall and Manuel (which are cited liberally in this writing) were some of my primary inspirations.

On September 11, 2001, terrorists crashed two airliners into the New York City World Trade Center Twin Towers and a third into the Pentagon, killing more than 2,500 and injuring many more. Apparently, other similar aborted attacks were directed at the nations' capital and other unknown destinations in the Washington, D.C. area. After the destruction of the Twin Towers and damage to the Pentagon, evidence of a spontaneous spiritual response was seen throughout America:

(1) Candlelight prayer and worship services sprang up in New York City among people of all races;

2) On Sunday, September 23, 2001, more than 30,000 gathered

in Yankee Stadium for a time of prayer and worship in which Christians, Muslims, and Jews joined together;

(3) In New York City, people of various races, cultures, and ethnic groups came together to express their respect for each other and their joint commitment to New York City and the nation;

(4) News reporters repeatedly used the phrase "this nation will never be the same;"

(5) President Bush, who has openly declared his Christian faith, called a national day of prayer for September 14, 2001;

(6) On September 14, churches throughout the nation were open, with many churches filled to capacity as Americans came together to pray, and clusters of citizens gathered for prayer on sidewalks in the cities.

God led me to focus upon the most important missing ingredient in America's response to God's call for America—the covenantal relationship between this nation and God. Our forefathers recognized this nation as a land of covenant, which is demonstrated repeatedly in America's early history:

• By the Declaration of Independence and Constitution and its Bill of Rights recognizing a covenant with God as a part of government's commitment to its citizens;

• By the Puritans who came to America to establish God's kingdom on earth, and were committed to a covenant with God, each other, and the land;

• By George Washington as he led this nation to independence and became its first president;

• By Benjamin Franklin, who did not claim to be a Christian, leading Congress to adopt the Constitution by declaring the "superintending providence in our favor," and that God governs in the "affairs of men;"

- By Jonathan Edwards, George Whitefield, Charles Finney, and Jeremiah Lanphier as they led America's eighteenth- and nineteenth-century spiritual awakenings;
- By Chief Justice John Marshall as he withstood the wrath of President Jefferson and Congress to establish the Supreme Court as the final arbitrator of the Constitution;
- By President Polk, congressmen, and other national leaders who declared the "manifest destiny" of America to extend from the Atlantic to the Pacific in the national debates over the Mexican War; and
- By Abraham Lincoln's declaration of a special covenantal relationship with God, spoken as a beacon light to the North and the South in the midst of America's Civil War.

Somewhere in its history, America lost that vision of one nation under God, a land of promise, a land of covenant. Now in the early twenty-first century, with events such as the September 11, 2001, attack, will we remember America's godly heritage?

Contemplating what he had written, the man lifted his voice to the Father, "Tell me more of your plans for America."

And the Father answered: "America was birthed as a national covenant between me, my Son, and this nation. That covenant was sealed on the cross, but it was also sealed by the blood of those who founded this nation. They set their faces like flint to establish a federation that was different than any other nation—a land of promise—a covenant nation—one nation under God. I have called it as a place for the ingathering of people of all races under the Lordship of my Son. I have called one nation under God. I have called this nation to demonstrate my glory in a republic that I have chosen and to prove that a nation may be established under the Lordship of my Son that will draw people from all countries, all cultures, and all ethnic groups to be one with my Son. You see the heart of America reflected in times of crisis. You see how quickly I can change things when people turn to me. I am in control of the destiny of this nation. It is my land—a land of covenant, a land of destiny, a land that I have chosen to demonstrate the Lordship of my Son in the world. I can heal divisions. I can perform quickly that which seems impossible to you. I bring victory out of what appears to be defeat. I am sovereign. There is no other. I rule in the affairs of men."

And now the journey begins.

Chapter 3

At a very early age I began to sail upon the ocean. For more than forty years, I have sailed everywhere that people go.

I prayed to the most merciful Lord about my heart's great desire, and He gave me the spirit and the intelligence for the task: seafaring, astronomy, geometry, arithmetic, skill in drafting spherical maps and placing correctly the cities, rivers, mountains and ports. I also studied cosmology, history, chronology and philosophy.

It was the Lord who put into my mind (I could feel His hand upon me) the fact that it would be possible to sail from here to the Indies. All who heard of my project rejected it with laughter, ridiculing me.

There is no question that the inspiration was from the Holy Spirit, because he comforted me with rays of marvelous illumination from the Holy Scriptures . . .
—from Christopher Columbus's *Book of Prophecies* [4]

THE CHRIST BEARER

The man visualized the birth of the Church in Jerusalem when the Crucified One, the Son of God, the Son of Man, Jesus, hung on the cross. The Church spread to the "outermost parts of the world," but primarily north through Laodicea, Sardis, Ephesus, Philadelphia, Pergamum, and other cities which are now located in Turkey and Greece, and finally through all of Europe.

In the early Church, the apostles, and particularly, Paul, continued the ministry begun by the Crucified One. Paul taught that the Kingdom of God was established through Jesus in the hearts of men. In Europe in the Middle Ages, the Church lost that vision of Jesus, the Suffering Servant, and ignored the fact that He was the head of the Church. A body of Christians was organized, which worshiped the Father, the Son, and the Holy Spirit in name only. Like the Scribes and Pharisees, these Christians "honored the Father with their lips, but their hearts were hard and their worship was only out of traditions and the words of men." (Isaiah 29:13–16) The Church created its own power—the power that dominated men. Utilizing the hates, fears, and lusts of its members to ensure that its power would endure, the Church developed intolerance to other opinions—not because it was confident of its faith, but because it was vulnerable. Conformity was mandatory.

Believers and non-believers expressed the distinguishing characteristic of the early Church, "See how they love one another." The distinguishing mark of the Church of the Middle Ages in Europe was its hierarchical arrogance and its quest for wealth and power. As the Church became more powerful, the Church leaders, rather than Jesus Christ, became the center of the Church of Europe. With this quest for power and authority, the Church plunged Europe into centuries of darkness and despair.

There were many true believers*⁵ in Europe who believed that the Son of God was to have preeminence. They suffered for their belief because they did not accept the authority of the Church. The witnessing and writings of many of these true believers brings light and inspiration to Christians to this day. Multitudes of Jews migrated from the land promised to Abraham throughout all of Europe. But despite the presence of these true believers and Jews, the Church of the Middle Ages, led by man and not by Jesus Christ, took dominion and authority over Europe.

The Church in Europe was established with the idea of Christian world dominion carried out by an assembly of cardinals, priests, and highly educated officials; but the Church leaders were motivated by greed and lost this vision. During the Middle Ages, the Church committed despicable acts in the name of God. The most grievous acts of the Church in Europe were directed toward three groups: infidels,*⁶ true believers, and Abraham's children. Perhaps the darkest days of the Church in the Middle Ages were the Crusades, which began in 1097 and continued periodically for approximately 200 years. Jerusalem was then under the control of the Turks, and Christendom believed it was called to liberate Israel from the "infidel" in the East. The Crusades were led by church and military leaders from Europe, and were principally directed toward Jerusalem. The First Crusade, which was called the "people's crusade," sought to "liberate" Jerusalem. The Crusaders came by diverse routes from France, Normandy, Flanders, England, Southern Italy, Sicily, and other places in Europe. An early crusade to Antioch and Jerusalem was described as follows:

---

*⁵ The term "true believers" as used in my text refers to those who seek to follow the teachings of Jesus as demonstrated by the early Church.

*⁶ The term "infidels" refers both to those who did not believe in Christian doctrine and also to those who expressed and practiced a faith different than the teaching of the established Church.

After a little more than a month's siege, the city (Jerusalem) was finally captured (July 15, 1099). The slaughter was terrible; the blood of the conquered ran down the streets, until men splashed in blood as they rode. At nightfall, "sobbing for excess of joy," the crusaders came to the Sepulchre from their treading of the winepress, and put their blood-stained hands together in prayer. So, on that day of July, the First Crusade came to an end.[7]

Eventually, whenever a Pope quarreled with someone or sought to weaken the power of another, he called for a Crusade.[8] Before the Crusades finished, the sword was extended to Abraham's children and the true believers. During one Crusade, it was reported that more than 15,000 "infidels" were murdered.[9]

The thirteenth century saw the development of the papal inquisitions, which were directed against the "heretics" who refused to follow the traditions of the Church. The well-known Spanish Inquisitions followed, resulting in the death or imprisonment of many true believers. The spirit of the Inquisitions was captured by the words of Pope Boniface VIII. In 1300, he issued the following pronouncement:

Both are in the power of the church, the spiritual sword, and the material. But the latter is to be used for the church, the former by her. . . . If, therefore, the earthly power err, it shall be judged by the spiritual power. . . . But if the spiritual power err, it can only be judged by God, not by man. . . . For this authority, though given to a man and exercised by a man, is not human, but rather divine . . . Furthermore, we declare, state, define, and pronounce that it is altogether necessary to salvation for every human creature to be subject to the Roman pontiff.[10]

In the marketplaces of Europe, many true believers were burned for their stands for truth or against the practices of the Church. One outspoken critic of the Church was John Wycliffe (1320–1384). Wycliffe was a learned doctor at Oxford and an outspoken critic of the corruption of the Church. He organized a number of priests called the Wycliffites to minister throughout England. So that the people could understand God's Word for themselves without having to rely on a priest's interpretation, Wycliffe translated the Bible into English. Although leaders of the church raged against him and ordered him imprisoned, he died a free man. But by decree of the Council of Constance in 1415, his remains were dug up and burned.[11]

The Church extended this spiritual darkness throughout the Middle Ages. A legal system controlled by priests regulated the lives of individuals throughout Europe in the eleventh, twelfth, and thirteenth centuries, giving the clergy almost total sovereignty. In the twelfth century, royal justice, administered by kings in cooperation with the clergy, was in place throughout Europe. The kings of Europe began to take charge of the legal system and learned to use and manipulate the papal, legal, and administrative techniques. Thus, by the fifteenth century, the Church was protected by the state, but was captivated by it and used as its instrument.[12] In order to pacify the Church, many European kings permitted it to exercise dominion over those three groups that it hated the most—infidels, true believers, and Jews. Therefore, the Church of Europe, which was called the cradle of Christianity, lost its great opportunity to become a haven for true believers.

There were many clerics and true believers who envisioned a nation in which Jesus was prominent. When their vision was not shared by the predominant Church, they were forced to move to remote areas of Europe or to hide from authorities in order to express their faith. In Moses' day, the cry of the Hebrews reached to the heavens, and God called Moses to deliver them to the land of promise. In the fifteenth century, the cry of the persecuted true believers for freedom also reached up to heaven, and God provided a new deliverer.

The Father's man for the moment was Christopher Columbus. The name Christopher means the "Christ bearer." Since Jesus Christ brought light to the world, the name Christopher has come to mean the "light bearer." He was a man chosen by God to introduce to Europe the new land of promise. A man without a single country, Columbus was born in Genoa, Italy, but he sailed under flags of many nations and developed close, personal ties with the crowns of England, France, and Burgundy. Thus, he was qualified to introduce to all of Europe this new land of promise.[13]

Columbus believed that he could travel to the West and open trade routes to the Indies. The Indies and other lands of the East had a reputation for great wealth, but the East was under the dominion of the Muslims. Columbus also believed that the trade routes would help to assist in the liberation of the Holy Lands from the grip of the Muslim horde.[14] He was intrigued by at least two strange signs: (1) pieces of carved driftwood with strange markings and (2) the bodies of two Chinese-looking men, which washed up near Azores. Christopher believed he had a special mission from God to spread the Gospel to undisclosed lands.[15]

Columbus calculated that it was 2,400 miles from the Canary Islands west to Japan. Portugal was the great seafaring nation of Columbus's day, and he had sailed for that nation many times. Therefore, Columbus first presented his plan to King John II, of Portugal. His proposal was rejected when the King's mathematician correctly calculated that it was a 10,000-mile journey westward to Japan.[16]

Christopher Columbus then went to the courts of Spain to plead for authority and provision to travel to the West in search of a new land. Finally, after hearing Christopher's plea, King Ferdinand and Queen Isabella of Spain accepted his appeal and sent him on his way. The Queen even offered her personal jewelry as collateral to help finance the expedition.[17]

Christopher solicited ships and men to travel with him to the West. Some followed Christopher with a vision for freedom. Others followed with a spirit for adventure. Soon, Christopher, the light bearer, located the men who were willing and able to journey with him across the great ocean. Finally, he obtained three ships for his journey. Before his journey, God planted in his heart the words of the prophet Isaiah:

Listen to me, O coastlands, and harken ye peoples from far; The Lord hath called me from the womb; from the body of my mother has he made mention of my name. I will also give thee for a light to the nations that thou mayest be my salvation unto the end of the earth. (Isaiah 49:1,6) [18]

Christopher's three ships left the port of Spain and traveled toward the West until they entered the great Atlantic Ocean. The steady winds and gentle ocean pushed them forward. Day after day, month after month, they traveled, always westward, a few hundred miles, then a thousand, two thousand miles, and then three thousand and more. Finally, the captains of the other ships informed Christopher that they faced mutiny if they continued their journey and demanded that Christopher turn back. Even the men on Christopher's ship threatened mutiny if he refused to give up.[19]

Christopher negotiated three more days in exchange for his promise to turn back on the third day. Then he went to the cabin to pray that the journey could be fulfilled. The first day they traveled an astonishing distance of fifty-nine leagues. The sailors were first frightened because they were widening their distance from their homeland, but then heartened when debris was found, indicating that land was nearby. Then, at 2:00 AM, with less than four hours remaining before the dawn of the third and final day, the cry came from a watchman on the Pinta that land had been sighted.[20]

They first arrived on an island, which they named San Salvador, meaning Holy Savior. There they met friendly natives who were curious about these new visitors but received them warmly. Christopher's attention quickly focused on the golden ornaments hung around the natives' necks. He was told of an island to the south called Babeque, where the inhabitants collected nuggets of gold on the beach by firelight and hammered them into bars. Columbus made his way toward Babeque, but bad weather forced him back to a larger island, which they named Española. They were shipwrecked at a place that they named La Navidad for the nativity. There they found the gold that they had searched for, which included masks, bracelets, necklaces, and rings. Then Christopher returned home, leaving thirty-nine men at La Navidad.[21]

Soon Columbus and his men sailed to the West on a second trip across the ocean. To their dismay, when they arrived at La Navidad, they found that all thirty-nine crewmen had been killed, and the once-friendly natives were now hostile. They learned that the crewmen had taken the native Indian women, not only one each but many, thus enraging the Indian men. Christopher and his men were no longer welcome in La Navidad.[22]

Columbus and his crew explored several islands south of Florida and points on the north coast of South America, where they discovered some gold, but no great deposits as they had anticipated. In the process, Columbus ignored the lust of his crewmen when they took native women for their pleasure. However, many of the women carried a disease known as syphilis, which the sailors introduced to Europe when they returned.[23]

Columbus virtually enslaved the natives, requiring that they pay a tribute of gold or be punished. Since there were no mines or fields in Española, the natives had to pan for whatever gold they could find. Eventually, the natives turned hostile. In two years, 100,000 of the approximately 300,000 natives of Española died or were killed, and by twelve years later, only 20,000 of the natives remained alive. Many of Columbus's crew died of fevers. And so Columbus and his crew returned to Spain in disgrace.[24]

Columbus ultimately received permission and funding from Spain for another trip to the Americas. His travels led him to the coast of South America, to what are now Honduras, Nicaragua, and Costa Rica, where he finally found the source of gold that had previously eluded him. Here, the natives led Columbus and his men to fields where the gold was located on the surface of the ground. This discovery brought destruction to the natives because the gold enticed Cortez, Pizarro, and thousands of conquistadors to come to America resulting in one of the bloodiest rapes of a country the world had ever known.[25]

Columbus returned home with his boats loaded with gold and visions of fame and wealth. But his return was overshadowed by the impending death of Queen Isabella, and Christopher did not receive the attention he thought he deserved. His last days were spent with his health ruined and sanity nearly gone, complaining because he had not received his share of the gold brought back to Spain from the new land he had discovered.[26]

As the man pondered these events, the Father spoke. "I called him as the light bearer and called him to the land of promise, and he faithfully journeyed across the ocean. But his heart turned from me to gold. And, therefore, he fell short of his mission. I did not allow him to enter the land of promise. Nevertheless, his journey planted in others the call that I have for America as a light bearer to the world.

"Christopher came because I called him to be a light bearer to the new land of promise, but he and his companions planted in the Americas a spirit of greed and lawlessness which defined the Americas from that day forward.

"My call was on this new land to be a land of freedom like no other land on the earth. As you continue your journey, I will show you more of my call and my plans for this new promised land."

Chapter 4

So the Lord said to him (Abram), "Bring me a heifer, a goat
and a ram, each three years old, along with a dove and a
young pigeon." Abram brought all these to him, cut them
in two and arranged the halves opposite each other; the
birds, however, he did not cut in half. Then birds of prey
came down on the carcasses, but Abram drove them away. . . .

When the sun had set and darkness had fallen, a smoking
fire pot with a blazing torch appeared and passed between
the pieces. On that day the Lord made a covenant with
Abram and said, "To your descendants I give this land . . ."
—Genesis 15:9–11 and 17–18, NIV

THE COVENANT

When Christopher returned to Spain from his trips to the Americas, he carried with him gold taken from the natives in the north coastal region of South America. News of Christopher's journeys spread, and men and women in all countries of Europe cast their eyes to the West. The discovery of the Americas shifted the center of gravity of the known world, ending the Crusades and the Middle Ages. All of the attention of Europe was now focused on this New World.[27]

Many adventurers in Spain and other countries of Europe looked to the new continent to fulfill their dreams of fortune, fame, and gold. But the true believers also looked to the West and thanked God for his faithfulness in providing a place of refuge. They petitioned God that it would be the new promised land, for which they had prayed so many years.

The two countries that came first were Spain and Portugal. The Spaniards mobilized their government to take dominion over the land and enlisted the Church to "convert" the natives.[28] However, the primary motivating force for the Spaniards was the gold of South America and other exaggerated claims of gold deposits all over the newly-discovered land. Spain and Portugal moved quickly to establish new colonies that would give them a stronghold in the New World. Portugal was the largest seafaring nation of that day. The Portuguese established settlements on the coast of Africa where they engaged in extensive slave trading. The Portuguese then developed Brazil into a slave colony.[29]

In addition to their conquest of territories of South America, the Spaniards, led by Cortez, conquered the Aztec Indians of Mexico and extended Spanish dominion north to California and other territories of what would later become the United States.

Since France and England were busy at home, with the French embroiled in a religious war with the Protestants, and England at war with the Irish, those nations did not participate in the first settlement of the West. Had France or England moved at that time to settle North America, the Spaniards undoubtedly would have tried to get to the land of promise first. But since France and England were not on the scene, Spain was free to harvest the wealth of South America.[30]

Because of true, but exaggerated, reports of gold in South America and false reports of gold in Florida, the Spaniards traveled to those two destinations. When the Spaniards arrived in Florida, they were soon driven out by the unfriendly climate, disease, and warring Indians,[31] although they did manage to establish a fort named San Marcos in east Florida and a second fort named San Michel in west Florida. Thus, by God's divine providence, North America was spared an onslaught of the armies of Spain and dominion of the Spanish Church. God had other plans for North America.

The natives of South America were very religious people with an appreciation of the supernatural and easily manipulated by people claiming to come in the name of God. The Spanish Church impoverished the people by taking the land's wealth and using their tithes and gifts to build great cathedrals and other church structures. By the end of the colonial days, the Church owned an estimated one-half of the wealth of the Latin American nations.[32]

Although the Spaniards conquered the Southwest, they did not come to North America with that same spirit of conquest. They were few in number and unorganized and spread out over the vast southwestern area of North America. While the Spanish Church came to South America with pomp, arrogance, and the manifest purpose of establishing a religious stronghold in the new land, the dominant Christian influence of the Spaniards in the Southwest area of North America was from the Franciscan and Dominican monks. These monks, accompanied by conquistadors, came to North America as humble servants with a loving commitment to the native people and the land. They traveled over areas of the Southwest, predominantly Texas, the New Mexico territory, and California. With their devotion to Jesus Christ and loving commitment to the natives, they established churches and converted natives in each area they visited. Sacrificially, they dedicated themselves to the land and to the natives.[33]

The French Jesuits also came to North America across eastern Canada and the northern United States to the Great Lakes, and later all the way south down the Mississippi River to the Gulf of Mexico. Through their zeal and devotion to the service of Christ and sacrificial living, the light of Christ was introduced by the Jesuits to the natives in America.[34]

The Spanish and French monks committed their lives to this new land as living examples of the Suffering Servant. Most of them died in the rugged land or at the hand of the warring native tribes. Their blood was poured out as a love offering for the Native Americans and for the land.

The first English colony was established in the early 1600s when 144 men, including one preacher named Robert Hunt, set out by ship for the new country. After a long journey, they arrived at Cape Henry, Virginia. When they went ashore, their first act was to erect a cross on the Virginia beach and kneel near the cross as Robert Hunt led a prayer dedicating the travelers and this new land to the Lord. The small group of Englishmen then founded Jamestown, the first English settlement in the new land. On the journey to America, these Englishmen had consumed almost all of their food and were ill-prepared for life in this rugged land. As a result of infectious disease and starvation, most of the settlers died in the first few months. When their spiritual leader, Robert Hunt, died in the first winter, the Jamestown settlement soon lost its sense of a covenant relationship with God. When other Englishmen came, they experienced the same high death rate resulting from disease and starvation. Jamestown struggled for existence until the production of tobacco, America's first cash crop, provided financial stability to the Virginia area.[35]

Others came to America looking for a place to worship the Father without the restraints of the European Church. The Pilgrims traveled to America and landed at Cape Cod bay where they established a settlement called Plymouth. Their journey to the new land was difficult because they were required to remain in the hull of the ship, and they experienced relentless ridicule by the sailors. Despite violent weather and food shortages, they survived the journey. Their constant prayer and trust in God protected them from the rough ocean and changed the hearts of the sailors, who began to realize that God heard the prayers of these strange people.[36]

Like the settlers at Jamestown, they were not prepared for the rough land and hard winters. During the first winter each settler had only five kernels of corn per day. In God's divine providence, they were rescued by two English-speaking Native American Indians—Samoset and Squanto—who taught them how to fish, hunt, and plant corn and also helped them establish peaceful relationships with the neighboring Indian tribes. (Samoset had learned his English from fishing captains who had fished the Maine shore. Squanto had been captured by Captain George Weymouth and had been taken to England with other Indians, where he was taught English. Miraculously they appeared on the scene when the Pilgrims needed them the most.) In the most difficult winter, despite near starvation, God sustained the Pilgrims.[37] Unlike Jamestown, those who settled at Plymouth demonstrated their faith and trust in God. The Pilgrims, although small in number, introduced the light of Christ to this new promised land.

Then came the Puritans. They, too, sought religious freedom, but came with a mission to establish God's kingdom on Earth. They were committed to establishing a working Christian society beyond the reach of the European Church, and considered the new nation to be the perfect opportunity to demonstrate this divine plan. They, more than any others, laid the foundation for a Christian nation in America. When they came to America, they made a covenant with their God, each other, and the land.[38]

The man pondered all of these events with one question, "Father, tell me what you have done in this early history of America." The Father answered, "I heard the cries for freedom in Europe and other parts of the world as I had heard the cry of Abraham's children in Pharaoh's land. Before Columbus set sail for the Americas, I called America as a special nation, a land of freedom like no other. Because Columbus and those from Spain and Portugal who followed him fixed their eyes on gold and sought domination of the new land, I diverted them from the land of promise.

"Others came to America with the same attitude of domination, but they were not organized and did not threaten the new land. I watched all who came, but my eyes were fixed on the Spanish and French monks who gave their lives for the love of the native people and poured out their blood as a commitment to the land. When Robert Hunt knelt on the ocean shore and dedicated this land to me, I made a covenant with him and this land. My eyes were fixed on the Pilgrims and the Puritans and others who committed their lives to this land. I was there when they journeyed to this land and when they struggled to survive. I observed their struggles and was with them as they died. I was there when they committed their lives to this nation and to me.

"I made a covenant with them. Even though many of their descendants have forgotten that covenant, I will never forget it; for that covenant was made between my Son and me and sealed by their blood.

"Continue your journey, my son, and I will unfold, even though through a glass dimly, my covenant plan for this nation."

Chapter 5

*It was wonderful to see the change soon made in the
manners of our inhabitants. From being thoughtless
or indifferent about religion, it seemed as if all the
world were growing religious, so that one could not
walk thro' the town in an evening without hearing
psalms sung in different families of every street.*

*Life, like a dramatic piece, should . . . finish handsomely.
Being now in the last act, I began to cast about for
something fit to end with . . . I sometimes wish, that you and I were
jointly employ'd by the Crown to settle a
colony on the Ohio . . . to settle in that fine country a
strong body of religious and industrous people! . . .
Might it not greatly facilitate the introduction of pure
religion among the heathen, if we could, by such a
colony, show them a better sample of Christians than
they commonly see in our Indian traders?*
—Writings of Benjamin Franklin about and to George Whitefield,
concerning his preaching in the colonies.[39]

THE SEED OF A NATION

When the Puritans ended their journey, they entered into the Mayflower Compact—a covenant to adopt a government of the people under God. During the time of Robert Hunt and the first Pilgrims and Puritans, a vision was planted that this land was truly destined to be one nation under God. The first settlers knew they would face hardships when they came to the New World, but they came with a commitment to freedom. When many of the settlers died during the cruel winters, the surviving settlers resolved that those deaths would not be in vain. At the end of each winter, the survivors had the choice to stay and commit their lives to this New World or return to the comfort of their motherland. Few returned. Almost all chose to stay, even with the threat that the next winter, Indian attack or plague would result in death. Our forefathers were willing to pour out their lives as a sacrifice because of their commitment to freedom.

America soon became a wealthy new place. Although it was a rough, cruel land, it offered a diversity of provision and opportunity that drew enterprising Englishmen and other Europeans to its shores. Trade companies and fleets of ships transported the beaver skins, hides, and other riches of America to Europe. For the first time, but not the last, the people of this new territory were in danger of losing their souls because of the astonishing wealth of the land. The first settlers dedicated the land to God and planted a vision of one nation under God. With their stomachs full and prosperity everywhere, the settlers soon decided that they didn't need God—they could handle things by themselves.

More than a century passed, and an attitude of pride and self-sufficiency soon developed. Because they had to battle the cruel hard terrain and the Indian tribes, the settlers soon developed a fiercely independent nature, which ultimately led to an attitude of lawlessness.

Meanwhile, the model for a new nation committed to God was planted in the heart of a young Englishman. At twelve years of age, William Penn was dramatically converted and his life was radically changed when he began to fellowship with the Quakers. He shared their desire to go to the New World to escape the religious persecution in England. This fellowship continued despite the resistance of his father, Sir William Penn, a wealthy English vice admiral, who would not tolerate his son's association with the Quakers.[40]

But William Penn was not deterred from his pursuit of religious freedom and his participation in the Quakers' religious activities. The Church of England would not tolerate itinerant preachers. Penn was arrested six times and sent to prison for preaching the Gospel from street corners. Penn's father saw his son's determination, and began to admire Penn's commitment; upon the death of Sir William Penn, the young William Penn acquired the massive wealth of his father.

After his father's death, Penn negotiated the cancellation of a debt of 16,000-pounds owed to his father by King Charles II in exchange for 28,000,000 acres of land in the New World. As a part of the agreement, King Charles gave this land the name Pennsylvania.[41]

Penn called this new territory a "Holy Experiment" and wrote a constitution for it. The preamble of his constitution contained these statements:

> Everyone must submit himself to the governing authorities, for there is no authority except that which God has established (Romans 13:1); Government seems to me to be a part of religion itself, a thing sacred in its institutions and ends; Liberty without obedience is confusion, and obedience without liberty is slavery.[42]

During Penn's lifetime he committed himself to the territory and its people, including the American Indians, and planted the vision of a nation under God. Penn made treaties with, and was respected by, the Native Americans; but after his death, all of the treaties he made with the Native American Indians were strategically broken. It appeared that his vision of a "Holy Experiment" was completely forgotten. But God did not forget the sacrifice of his loyal servant William Penn.

God planted the preachers in this new land to keep the vision that He intended. In the New World, the preachers were the spiritual leaders, and each settlement was established around the church. The preacher also taught the children, administered the schools, and led or participated in all settlement government meetings. Even though the busy new Americans lost their vision of God's call, most of the preachers did not. And so the children were taught, the settlers heard from the pulpit, and in meetings of the settlement, the people were reminded that this was a land of equality—a land of freedom with a covenant relationship with God.

Nevertheless, after the passage of more than a century from the first settlement, the new Americans lost sight of God's plan. By 1700, the religious fervor, which had characterized many of the first settlements of the New World, had long since died away. In 1706, Dr. Cotton Mather asserted:

> It is confessed by all who know anything of the matter . . . that there is a general and an horrible decay of Christianity, among the professors of it . . . The modern Christianity is too generally but a very spectre, scarce a shadow of the ancient. Ah! sinful nation. Ah! children that are corrupters: what have your hands done! . . . So notorious is this decay of Christianity, that whole books are even now and then written to inquire into it.[43]

Then came the Great Awakening, and the winds of Heaven began to blow upon America. Between the years 1720 and 1735, several evangelical revivals took place. These are described by Arnold A. Dallimore in his two-volume biography of George Whitefield:

(1) There was a revival among the Germans in Pennsylvania, which included Lutherans, Reformed, Mennonites, Quakers, Moravians, Schwenkfelders, Dunkers (known as Baptists), and others who had settled in the rural areas northwest of Philadelphia and in a community named Germantown. Especially among the Mennonites and Baptists, powerful awakenings occurred, with many conversions.

(2) In the 1720s, Theodorus Frelinghuysen, minister for Dutch Reformed Churches in the wilderness country of the Raritan Valley of New Jersey, preached against the emptiness of the existing church and declared the absolute necessity of being born again. Although his teachings drew bitter opposition, his Christian character and his evangelical aggressiveness influenced other ministers of all denominations.

(3) In the early eighteenth century, Reverend William Tennent led the Presbyterian Church of America to a period of spiritual awakening.[44]

But the Great Awakening started in Jonathan Edwards's church in Northampton, Massachusetts. Joseph Tracy, in his outstanding writing *The Great Awakening: A History of the Revival of Religion in the time of Edwards and Whitefield,* describes the revival led by Jonathan Edwards. The next paragraphs extensively refer to Tracy's writings.

In the early 1730s, Edwards was concerned about the prevailing system that permitted the entrance of unconverted men into the ministry. To determine the fitness of a person for membership, the church looked at their good standing and the acts that they performed regardless of any experience of conversion. The prevailing view in the church held that a person who expected to be saved could be saved by his works, and that he must therefore be careful to do works by which he could expect to be saved. Preparation for Heaven could be put off to a more "convenient season."[45] There were many in the church who never had sought after or experienced a spiritual conversion, and the difference between the church and the world was diminishing. With the decline of true conversions came a laxity of morals.

Jonathan Edwards's sermons on justification by faith preached in 1734 to his congregation in Northampton, Massachusetts, set off the Great Awakening. Edwards announced that he intended to challenge the prevailing view that heaven could be attained by works. Influential friends endeavored to dissuade him but to no avail. His series of sermons entitled "Justification by Faith Alone" was based on the same argument that Luther declared to be the ultimate issue upon which the church stands. Through his sermons, Edwards intended to establish the truth that man can be justified before God by faith alone, and to sweep aside any hope that heaven could be attained by the works of man.[46]

In the latter part of December 1734, as Edwards preached at Northampton, "the Spirit of God began extraordinarily to set in and wonderfully to work among us; and there were very suddenly, one after another, five or six persons, who were, to all appearance, savingly converted, and some of them wrought upon in a very remarkable manner."[47]

One of the persons converted was a young woman who had had some notoriety as a leader "in scenes of gayety and rustic dissipation." News of her conversion spread like a flash of lightning;

many acknowledged the goodness of God which had produced such a change in her. Through Edwards's series of sermons . . .

> . . . the work of conversion was carried on in a most astonishing manner, and increased more and more. Souls did, as it were, come by flocks to Jesus Christ. From day to day, for many months together, there might be seen evident instances of sinners brought out of darkness into the marvellous light. Our public assemblies were then beautiful; the congregation was alive in God's service, every one earnestly intent on the public worship, every hearer eager to drink in the words of the minister as they came from his mouth.[48]

Reports of revival in Northampton spread to other towns, where many ridiculed it. However, great numbers who came to Northampton carried revival to their hometowns; the revival spread to Suffield, Sunderland, Deerfield, Hatfield, West Springfield, Long Meadow, Enfield, and other places. Soon the spirit of revival spread to Connecticut and New Jersey. In Edwards's view, the impact of his message on its listeners was "a conviction of the justice of God in their condemnation, a sense of their own exceeding sinfulness, and the vileness of all their performances."[49]

Edwards preached from an elevated pulpit above the people and read long sermons in a monotone. His eyes were either fixed on his writings or the back hall of the church, and he never looked at the people. Under the conviction of the words that he preached, the people cried out, sobbed, and fell to the floor during his long messages. On July 8, 1741, in Enfield, Connecticut, he preached his most famous sermon, "Sinners in the Hands of an Angry God." The sermon frightened the people beyond control; many convulsed in tears of agony and distress, while others cried in repentance.[50]

Edwards's writings mention twenty-five other places that experienced the work of God in the power of the Holy Spirit. He referred to this as "this remarkable outpouring of the Spirit of God which extended from one end to the other of this county."[51]

In the backwoods of Pennsylvania, Connecticut, and New Jersey, revival occurred among the Indians through the ministry of David Brainerd. Brainerd, a Presbyterian minister, was in open awe of the power of God, which fell on one village after another as he preached. The Indians were dramatically converted, and skeptical white settlers were also instantly converted. Brainerd often preached three times a day, with each sermon lasting for hours. He died of tuberculosis at the age of twenty-nine. John Wesley said of Brainerd: "Find preachers of David Brainerd's spirit, and nothing can stand before them . . . Let us be followers of him, as he was of Christ, in absolute self-devotion, in total deadness to the world, and in fervent love to God and man."[52]

But the primary instrument used by God to bring revival to the new land was a young Englishman named George Whitefield. Whitefield was a good friend of John Wesley and a member of Wesley's "Holy Club." At age twenty-two he started his ministry in England. In city after city in England, revival broke out following his sermons. Because of the jealousy of the ministers, the churches were soon closed to Whitefield, and he took his messages to the streets and countryside, where thousands and tens of thousands often listened to his two- or three-hour sermons.

Whitefield's determination to preach the Gospel was profoundly influenced before he came to America by his open-air ministry to the poor people of Bristol. He spoke of the green Bristol countryside covered with piles of coal, squalid huts, and deep semi-circles of unwashed faces:

The first discovery of their being affected was to see the white gutters made by their tears which plentifully fell down their black cheeks, as they came out of their coal pits. Hundreds and hundreds of them were soon brought under deep convictions, which, as the event proved, happily ended in a sound and thorough conversion. The change was visible to all, though numbers chose to impute it to anything, rather than the finger of God.[53]

The ministry of Wesley, Whitefield, and other members of the "Holy Club" brought about a spiritual transformation of England and prevented a revolution like the French Revolution. The same spiritual transformation followed Whitefield's ministry in America. Whitefield learned from Wesley of the preaching opportunities in America; from then on, America was the primary place for Whitefield to preach.

Following the revivals led by Jonathan Edwards, the people of the colonies were stirred by news from England of Whitefield's ministry in the churches of Bristol and London and his even greater works in the open-air meetings. Then the word came that Whitefield was on his way to the colonies and that he would arrive in Philadelphia.[54] Whitefield first spoke in Philadelphia on Friday evening, November 2, 1739. His first open-air meeting was on the following Thursday. Although it was late autumn and the days were getting cold, he preached from the courthouse steps to about 6,000 people. On Friday, Saturday, and Sunday, the crowds increased to approximately 8,000.[55]

Whitefield went from one town or village to another in the new land preaching two or three two-hour sermons a day. The settlers saw the minister riding horseback from one town to another at all hours of the day or night. Often a rider recognized Whitefield journeying by horseback, and asked him where he was going. When Whitefield told him his destination, the rider rode ahead at full speed letting everyone know, "Whitefield is coming." Then around the meeting place, a cloud of dust and quake of the ground were evident as thousands of wagons and horses raced to the place where Whitefield was to preach. A farmer named Nathan Cole added his description of the excitement generated by Whitefield's preaching:

> Now it pleased God to send mr whitefield into this land & . . . i longed to see & hear him . . . & then one morning all on a Suding there came a messanger & said mr whitefield . . . is to preach at middletown this morning at 10 o=clock i was in my field at work i dropt my tool that i had in my hand & run home and throu my house and bad my wife to get ready quick to go and hear mr whitefield preach at middletown & run to my pastire for my hors with all my might fearing i should be too late to hear him & took up my wife & went forward as fast as i thought ye hors could bear & when my hors began to be out of breth i would get down and put my wife on ye saddel and bid her ride as fast as she could & not Stop or Slack for me except i bad her & so i would run until i was almost out of breth & then mount my hors again . . . fearing we should be too late to hear ye Sarmon for we had twelve miles to ride dubble in little more than an our. . . . i saw before me a cloud or fog i first thought of from ye great river but as i came nearer ye road i heard a noise something like a low rumbling thunder & i presently found out it was ye rumbling of horses feet coming down ye road & this Cloud was a Cloud of dust made by the running of horses feet it arose some rods into ye air over the tops of ye hills and trees & when i came

within about twenty rods of ye road i could see men and
horses slipping along . . . & when we gat down to ye old
meeting hous thare was a great multitude it was said to be
3 or 4000 & when i looked towards ye great river i see ye fery
boats running swift forward and backward . . . [56]

The impact of Whitefield's ministry was demonstrated by
Cole's final words:

. . . when I see mr whitefield come up upon ye scaffold he
looked almost angellical a young slim slender youth before
thousands of people and with a bold undainted countenance
& my hearing how god was with him everywhere as he came
along it solemnized my mind and put me in a trembling fear
before he began to preach for he looked as if he was Clothed
with authority from ye great god and a sweet solemnity sat
upon his brow and my hearing him preach gave me a heart
wound & by gods blessing my old foundation was broken up
and I see my righteousness would not save me.[57]

Whitefield's second campaign in America, which began in
1740 shortly after his twenty-sixth birthday, was called by historian
Edwin Scott Gaustad "the greatest single evangelical tour in New
England's history."[58] In Boston, during that campaign, he addressed
over 15,000, which was approximately the city's population.[59]

In his biography of Whitefield, Dallimore reports:

. . . so numerous were the converts throughout the Colonies
that many Christians actually began to believe the millennium
was coming. Such a prophecy as . . . the earth shall be full

of the knowledge of the Lord, as the waters cover the sea which had formerly seemed all but impossible of fulfillment, now took on an exciting new reality in the minds of these people; now they could see that the Revival well might spread till it reached every nation and till all mankind were converted, and they believed that to a world made righteous the Saviour would then return to reign.[60]

Whitefield ministered in New England, including New York en route back to Georgia, during which he was challenged by and contended against the "unconverted ministry." Whitfield repeatedly expressed the view that Edwards was preaching that a person must be born again to minister for the Lord and enter into the Kingdom of God. As a result, many ministers and students of the ministry were converted.[61]

Whitefield returned to England, where he remained for approximately four years. During that time, the revival continued under the ministry of many other able preachers and spread further into the life of the colonies, particularly in New England. Gilbert Tennent continued Whitefield's ministry in New England. With reference to the result of Whitefield and Tennent's ministries in Boston, the Reverend Thomas Prince, Senior, said:

In this year 1741, the very face of the town (Boston) seemed to be strangely altered. Some who had not been here since the fall before, have told me of their great surprise at the change in the general look and carriage of the people. . . . I knew many of these had been greatly affected, and were now formed into religious societies.[62]

Through the preaching of Whitefield, God united the colonies in ways that few people would have expected, as

Presbyterians, Episcopals, Catholics, Quakers, and Moravians all accepted the same Christ in the same way.[63] Together, they began to discover a basic truth, which would be the major foundation stone of God's new nation and a primary cornerstone of the Revolution of 1776—that in the eyes of the Creator, all men are created equal. By the sovereign act of Almighty God through the obedience of Edwards, Whitefield, and other dedicated ministers, the Body of Christ was forming into one body in America that could stand firm in the days of the Revolution, and the concept of one people under God began to unite the people as one nation under God.

Because of Whitefield's ministry, the thirteen colonies were united on a spiritual level that none would have anticipated. In New England, with a 1760 estimated population of 502,000 people, converts were estimated in excess of 50,000.[64] From the pulpits of the churches—Episcopal, Catholic, Congregational, Presbyterian, and Moravian—the message of the risen Christ rang throughout the New World. For more than a century, the circuit-riding preachers, following the lead of Whitefield, spread the light of the Gospel of Christ across America, riding horseback across the roads of the colonies, often sleeping on the horse, and traveling on to their next preaching destination.

The man pondered all of these events and remembered how soon the vision of our forefathers was forgotten. Why have we, as a nation, forgotten the tremendous sacrifices of our forefathers for the right to worship and live in a free land?

The man remembered the thousands of Native American Indians who trusted these new settlers because they believed that words spoken by a man came from his soul and must be true. The man thought of the betrayal and murder of these Native Americans. He remembered how they were dispossessed of the lands, even land given to them through treaties, and were ultimately forced onto reservations. The man wondered how a country whose founders poured out their lives to establish a noble nation under God could soon forget their forefathers' sacrifices. But then he observed how quickly things can change through the ministry of men like Edwards, Brainerd, and Whitefield.

As the man pondered these events, he lifted his eyes to his Heavenly Father and said "Father, why are you taking me on this journey? What do you intend to teach me?"

And the Father replied, "Hear the lessons from my Word. I called Abraham from the land of Ur to a land he did not know. And he came and he trusted me and I made a covenant with him. That covenant was the seed of a nation. I have never forgotten that covenant.

"I called your forefathers to this new land of promise, and they came and they poured out their lives for this land, and I made a covenant with them which is the seed of this nation.

"You know how I raised up Moses and Joshua and David and raised up preachers and prophets like Samuel, Elijah, Elisha, and Isaiah. You now see how I have prepared preachers in the land to carry out my plans and purposes. A part of your journey will be to identify the Moseses and Joshuas and Davids and the prophets and teachers like Elijah, Elisha, and Isaiah that I have raised up in this land. The rest of your journey will be to see the purposes for which I have called them and the covenant relationship that I have made through them with this land."

Chapter 6

*It cannot be emphasized too strongly or too often that this
great nation was founded, not by religionists, but by Christians;
not on religions, but on the Gospel of Jesus Christ.
For this very reason peoples of other faiths have been
afforded asylum, prosperity, and freedom of worship here.*
—Patrick Henry, in May of 1765 [65]

*For my own part I consider it as nothing less
than a question of freedom or slavery . . . It is only
in this way that we can hope to arrive at truth, and
fulfill the great responsibility which we hold to
God and our country . . .*

*Is life so dear, or peace so sweet, as to be purchased
at the price of chains and slavery? Forbid it,
Almighty God! I know not what course others
may take; but as for me, give me liberty or give me death!*
—Patrick Henry, on March 23, 1775 [66]

THE CRUCIBLE OF FREEDOM

The Puritans, Penn, and other settlers planted a vision of a people of freedom governed by free men in a covenant relationship with their heavenly Father. As Whitefield rode horseback across the thirteen colonies preaching more than 18,000 sermons between 1739 and 1770, a spirit of unity was formed in the churches of this new land. The Father in heaven, remembering the covenant with the forefathers of this nation, extended the same vision of freedom and equality for all of its citizens. The cry of "freedom, justice, and equality" rang in the hearts of the settlers.

These new Americans who came to this country to escape religious intolerance and persecution insisted on the equality of all believers; the preachers and Christians went from the churches to the meeting places and assemblies and secured this vision of equality. The seed of a nation was contained in the concept that all men were created by their heavenly Father, and that He desires that they live in unity of purpose and commitment. The settlers began to sense that life in America was different than in the motherland. Here each man could pursue his own dreams in freedom; and yet, people could unite with their friends and neighbors in a common commitment to each other and the land. Their dream was to join together to conquer the land and not, as was so often the case in the nations from which they came, to conquer each other. The seed of revolution was the vision of a New World where men could live together and work together in liberty. The cry of "freedom" and "liberty" which brought their forefathers to this land now sounded in the hearts of these Americans.

We hold these truths to be self-evident, that all men are created equal; that they are endowed by their Creator with certain inalienable rights; that among these are life, liberty and the pursuit of happiness; that to secure these rights, governments are instituted . . .

These words were written in the hearts of the settlers before they were penned by Jefferson. The events leading to the Declaration of Independence, as well as the words of the Declaration itself, cemented the will and resolve of citizens of all colonies to do what was necessary to establish such a government. Never before in the history of the world have any people established a new nation with such a noble idea of the equality of men. From the influence upon Jefferson of Greek philosophers in the drafting of the Declaration of Independence, as well as the Christian heritage, came the concept of a land of liberty with a moral compass founded upon an "infinite being."

England, by its military presence, oppressive taxation, and efforts to require this nation to submit to the King, brought the colonists to the point of revolution. But the Americans, in their hearts, were ready to revolt. The cry of Patrick Henry, "Give me liberty, or give me death," reflected the resolve of Americans in all thirteen colonies.

And thus came revolution, and out of it, the birth of a new nation.

For several years leading up to 1776, the thirteen colonies were stirred with indignation because of the oppressive acts of the Englishmen. The spirit of independence was declared from one colony to another.[67] But to be free, the colonies had to take a stand against an English empire built upon the most massive military and naval forces the world had ever seen.

The English determined that revolution must be aborted by force and in April 1775 moved part of their military force against the Americans at Lexington and Concord. The Americans heard of their coming. During the night, Paul Revere and other pony express riders rode throughout the countryside warning the villagers and farmers that the British were coming. The British, who expected the resurgence to end overnight, met with surprising resistance and were amazed at the efficiency and determination of the minutemen. Shouts of "freedom" and "victory" rang throughout the countryside, as the minutemen proved to all of the colonies that they could stand against the British forces.[68]

On July 4, 1776, the Second Continental Congress declared America's independence. The thought of independence in this new land appeared as a dream to the rest of the world, and especially to the imperialistic Englishmen, who had conquered and controlled many other territories like America. How could a small number of Americans, spread over several colonies, without any unity or military force, with limited small handguns and powder and almost no other military weapons, expect to stand against the great English military might?

The military history of this new nation's fight for independence discloses God's divine provision carried out through the resolve of a man God raised up for the moment. That man was George Washington.

That Washington was alive was itself a miracle. Washington distinguished himself in the French and Indian Wars about twenty years before the Declaration of Independence. In the battle of Monongahela in July of 1755, as the last surviving officer on horseback, he became the object of fire from the Indians as he rode back and forth across the battlefield. Two horses were shot from under him, and four musket balls passed through his shirt, but he remained uninjured. Years later, an Indian chief told Washington and others the following:

I am a chief and ruler over my tribes. My influence extends
to the waters of the great lakes and to the far blue mountains.

I have traveled a long and weary path that I might see the young warrior of the great battle. It was on the day when the white man's blood mixed with the streams of our forests that I first beheld this chief. I called to my young men and said, mark yon tall and daring warrior? He is not of the red-coat tribe—he hath an Indian's wisdom, and his warriors fight as we do—himself alone exposed. Quick let your aim be certain, and he dies. Our rifles were leveled, rifles which, but for you, knew not how to miss—twas all in vain, a power mightier far than we, shielded you. Seeing you were under the special guardianship of the Great Spirit, we immediately ceased to fire at you. I am old and soon shall be gathered to the great council fire of my fathers in the land of shades, but ere I go, there is something bids me speak in the voice of prophecy: Listen! The Great Spirit protects that man [pointing at Washington], and guides his destinies—he will become the chief of nations, and a people yet unborn will hail him as the founder of a mighty empire. I am come to pay homage to the man who is the particular favorite of Heaven, and who can never die in battle.[69]

One famous Indian warrior also declared that, "Washington was never born to be killed by a bullet! I had seventeen fair fires at him with my rifle, and after all could not bring him to the ground!"[70]

Washington was a man of prayer who sought and witnessed God's divine intervention in the circumstances that led to the founding of this nation. When Washington took command of the Colonial Army, he found the army in disarray and with a lack of discipline. He issued general orders, which included the following:

The General most earnestly requires and expects a due observance of those articles of war established for the government of the army, which forbid profane cursing, swearing, and drunkenness. And in like manner, he requires and expects of all officers and soldiers not engaged in actual duty, a punctual attendance of Divine services, to implore the blessing of Heaven upon the means used for our safety and defense. . . .The General orders this day [July 20, the first national fast day] to be religiously observed by the forces under this Command, exactly in manner directed by the Continental Congress. It is therefore strictly enjoined on all officers and soldiers to attend Divine service. And it is expected that all those who go to worship do take their arms, ammunition, and accoutrements, and are prepared for immediate action, if called upon.[71]

Throughout the war, providence intervened at critical moments to deliver the colonial militia from what appeared to be certain defeat. When the militia was out of supplies or ammunition, more suddenly surfaced to sustain them for another day. On other occasions, the militia created their own weapons such as large "chandeliers"—sectional wooden frameworks designed to hold stones in place. The Americans filled barrels with stones and laid them end-to-end in front of the chandeliers. When the British arrived, the chandeliers were knocked loose, and the barrels were sent down into their ranks with devastating effect. On other occasions, inclement weather or fog permitted the colonial army to outmaneuver the British. When the British had control of Boston, "a wind more violent than any I'd ever heard" (written by a British soldier) caused the British army to withdraw. British General William Howe concluded that the delayed movement of the British army, as the result of the violent wind, had permitted the rebels to strengthen and solidify their position; and that the defense of Boston was therefore untenable. General Howe then withdrew from Boston without a fight.[72]

Two miracles exemplify the colonial victories. The first miracle happened on Manhattan Island, near Brooklyn, while Washington gathered his army. The Colonial Army of approximately 8,000, with half untrained men and limited arms, was trapped on Manhattan by a 15,000-man British army led by General Howe. The British troops were supported by the British naval forces, and additional British ground troops were on the way to support Howe. Washington's army appeared to have no chance to survive an onslaught by these impressive forces. Surprisingly, Howe stopped, waited, and did not follow up on his obvious advantage. This delay gave Washington an opportunity to regroup, but his army was still trapped on Manhattan Island.

Out of desperation, Washington devised a plan to deliver his army by small boats across the East River. The first thing needed was the small boats and men to handle them; miraculously, a group of expert oarsmen appeared on the scene with the necessary boats. During the night, the oarsmen made one trip after another across the East River, delivering Washington's army to safety. Miraculously, they were not heard or seen by the British Navy or ground forces, even though the skies were clear and the area moonlit. At dawn, a large part of the Colonial Army was still on the island when an unexpected dense fog settled over both encampments. The fog remained until the last boat, with Washington as a passenger, departed from the island. Because of Divine Intervention, there still was a Colonial Army.[73]

The second great miracle happened at Valley Forge in what is called the "Crucible of Freedom." Washington moved his army to

Valley Forge for the winter of 1778–79. The winter was extremely cruel; many died, and many others had limbs amputated because of the severe cold. Naked and starving soldiers were a constant sight. But every morning, Washington was seen by the soldiers riding from one group of men to the next. They could sense his fatherly concern and knew that he was a man of prayer, and the strength of his will and commitment to the cause of freedom sustained them.

The peril of the Continental Army was known throughout the land. The nation, led by pastors, committed itself to prayer, sensing the tremendous physical and spiritual struggle of Valley Forge. The miracle of Valley Forge manifested itself in the fact that the army survived the cruel winter, and in the manner in which the steel will and determination of Washington was written in the hearts and minds of the soldiers and the nation. The experience at Valley Forge set the face of a nation like flint to never bow until freedom was accomplished.

Although the fight for freedom lasted for more than two years after Valley Forge, the war was won in the national commitment of the soldiers and citizens and their leader, George Washington, in the winter at Valley Forge.[74]

The man lifted his eyes to the Father to see what the Father would tell him of these events that birthed a new nation, and the Father spoke. "This nation is the new land of promise. It was born out of struggle because the prince of this world knows my calling for this nation. Will this nation remember its history and the commitment of the early Americans for freedom? You look at these events from a perspective of 200 years later and see that the nation has forgotten so much of its early history. But remember, your perspective is only of the present and the past, but I see the future.

"Continue your journey and see what I will next show you."

Chapter 7

Almighty God; We make our earnest prayer that
Thou wilt keep the United States in Thy Holy protection;
and Thou wilt incline the hearts of the Citizens to cultivate
a spirit of subordination and obedience to Government;
and entertain a brotherly affection and love for one another
and for their fellow Citizens of the United States at large,
and particularly for their brethren who have served in the Field.

And finally that Thou wilt most graciously be pleased
to dispose us all to do justice, to love mercy, and to
demean ourselves with that Charity, humility, and pacific
temper of mind which were the Characteristics of the Divine
Author of our blessed Religion, and without a humble
imitation of whose example in these things we can
never hope to be a happy nation.

Grant our supplication, we beseech Thee,
through Jesus Christ our Lord. Amen.
—Concluding paragraphs in Washington's farewell letter
sent to the governors of the thirteen states, June 8, 1783. [75]

THE NOBLE EXPERIMENT

It took almost 300 years to write the United States Constitution. It was written as Columbus refused to turn back when the captains of the other ships demanded it and he faced mutiny on his ship.

It was written with the blood of the first settlers at Jamestown and in New England when many of them died in the cruel winters in this New World.

It was forged in the will of a nation as it watched Washington and his troops survive the cruel winter of Valley Forge.

But it was primarily written in the churches and secret meeting places of Christians in England and the newly established churches and schools in the New World. Since the church in the villages of the colonies was the primary meeting place and the source of education, the church had a dynamic influence on the adults and their children, and a profound influence on the framers of the Constitution. The principles of freedom, equality of man, freedom from tyranny, and religious freedom were planted in the soul of a nation before they were written by the founding fathers.

It would seem easy to reduce to paper what was clearly written in the heart of a nation, but this was not the case. Despite the unity of the colonies in their fight for independence, there appeared to be little sentiment for a central government. The biggest obstacle to a new government and its constitution was fear—fear of a king, fear of a central government, fear of the domination of an intolerant church, fear of a loss of freedom, and fear of a loss of the sovereignty of the colonies. In fact, some of the colonies were negotiating separate trade agreements with other countries in competition with other colonies.[76] Despite the common desire for freedom and brotherhood, the framing of a constitution was almost doomed from the beginning.

George Washington sent letters throughout the colonies pleading with leaders for something to be done to save the union. Out of his efforts came the Constitutional Convention in 1787. The meetings in Philadelphia were stormy and contentious. The Northern states insisted that representation be based on population. The Southern states insisted on state sovereignty. When it appeared that a compromise was impossible, the frail, elderly Benjamin Franklin, considered by some to be almost senile, sent his written message for presentation to the convention. Although he had openly proclaimed that he was not a Christian, he reminded the delegates of America's divine provision:

In the beginning of the contest with Britain, when we were sensible of danger, we had daily prayers in this room for Divine protection. Our prayers, Sir, were heard, and they were graciously answered. All of us who were engaged in the struggle must have observed frequent instances of a super-intending Providence in our favor . . . And have we now forgotten this powerful Friend? Or do we imagine we no longer need His assistance? . . . I have lived, Sir, a long time, and the longer I live, the more convincing proofs I see of this truth: 'that God governs in the affairs of man.' And if a sparrow cannot fall to the ground without His notice, is it probable that an empire can rise without His aid? . . . We have been assured, Sir, in the Sacred Writings that except the Lord build the house, they labor in vain that build it. I firmly believe this. I also believe that, without His con-curring aid, we shall succeed in this political building no better than the builders of Babel; we shall be divided by our little, partial local interests; our projects will be confounded; and we ourselves shall become a reproach and a byword down to future ages. And what is worse, mankind may hereafter, from this unfortunate instance, despair of establishing government by human wisdom and leave it to chance, war, or conquest . . . I therefore beg leave to move that, henceforth, prayers imploring the assistance of Heaven and its blessing on our deliberation be held in this assembly every morning before we proceed to business.

This speech brought the delegates to private sober reflection and prayer, which turned the tide. With Washington's leadership, the Constitution was adopted and later the Bill of Rights was ratified by the states.[77]

Britain's great prime minister of the nineteenth century, William Gladstone, called it "the most wonderful work ever struck off at a given time by the brain and purpose of man."[78] Sir Winston Churchill argued the connection between the American Constitution and English social tradition:

Yet behind it (the Constitution) lay no revolutionary theory. It was based not upon the challenging writings of the French philosophers, which were soon to set Europe ablaze, but on Old English doctrine, freshly formulated to meet an urgent American need. The Constitution was a reaffirmation of faith in the principles painfully evolved over the centuries by the English-speaking peoples. It enshrined long-standing English ideas of justice and liberty, henceforth to be regarded on the other side of the Atlantic as basically American.[79]

The Constitution created a central government, but balanced its power among the president, the congress, and the courts. It also balanced the representative rights among the most populous states, which had greater representation in the House of Representatives; states had equal representation in the Senate. But most important was the grant to the people of the inalienable rights first declared in the Declaration of Independence and later expressed in the Bill of Rights, which was adopted by the states as a part of the Constitution. The preamble to the Constitution, in its most glorious proclamation for all generations of Americans, declares its goals for government:

> We the people of the United States, in order to form a more perfect union, establish justice, insure domestic tranquility, provide for the common defense, promote the general welfare, and secure the blessings of liberty to ourselves and our posterity, do ordain and establish this Constitution for the United States of America.

The Constitution also provided for amendments, but only by a vote of the people of two-thirds of the states, thus assuring that the Constitution could be changed only through the deliberate will of the citizens of the states.

The man pondered God's divine intervention in the history of this nation from a perspective that he had never seen before. Truly the Father preserved this nation and led our forefathers to establish a nation based on the covenant that the Father made with them. Even though we as a nation may drift to the left or the right, when the people are ready, the Constitution, as an anchor, will permit our return to the promise of freedom that led our forefathers to shed their blood for it.

Then the man began to ponder the price of freedom. He remembered a Supreme Court justice, appointed for life, who arrogantly said, "The Constitution is what we say it is." He thought of the many court decisions that decreed freedom from the underlying Christian truths upon which this nation was founded. He could hear the cry of "freedom" ringing throughout this land in the last forty years: "We want freedom. We want to do what we want to do without restraint."

He thought of the many occasions when a servant of God expressed His truth to the nation, and he remembered the outcry of the press and the people against that servant of God because the nation was unwilling to accept the revelation of truth and its consequential restraints. Then the Father led the man to the words of Isaiah:

> These are rebellious people, deceitful children,
> children unwilling to listen to the
> Lord's instruction.
> They say to the seers,
> 'See no more visions!'
> and to the prophets,
> 'Give us no more visions of what is right!
> Tell us pleasant things,
> prophesy illusions.
> Leave this way,
> get off this path,
> and stop confronting us
> with the Holy One of Israel!'
> —Isaiah 30:9–11

And the man thought of the consequences of freedom in a country that is unwilling to accept God's truth or any other absolute declaration of right and wrong. The man remembered the millions of unborn babies put to death in this nation in the name of freedom.

Then the man lifted his heart to the Father and asked, "Is there any hope? Is the price of freedom too great? Is there any hope for America?"

And the Father spoke. "Remember, my son, that I know the price of freedom. I paid the price of freedom when I gave Adam and Eve the right to choose and watched as they delivered the whole earth to the prince of this world. I paid the price of freedom when I gave my Son to take away the sins of the world.

"Freedom must permit choices. As I gave Adam and Eve the right to choose, so I have established a whole nation founded upon freedom with the underlying right of the nation to choose its own destiny. The right to choose, even for a nation, must include the right to follow or reject me and to accept or reject my truths.

"There is a price to obtain freedom but a greater price to preserve it. And freedom that is not founded upon my truths will ultimately lead to oppression or anarchy.

"Continue your journey, my son. You have reached the beginning point of this nation and your journey now really begins."

Part 2

THE ESSENCE OF FREEDOM

**The strongest principle of growth
lies in human choice.**

—George Eliot, pen name for nineteenth-century
English writer Mary Anne Evans

Chapter 8

. . . they sailed for the New World in response to God's call on their lives to be a covenanted people under Him, and proof to the rest of the world that it was possible for men to live with one another in harmony. Through great trials and perils, they held on to that vision, and the Lord sustained them. Finally with victory in the War for Independence, America had won her freedom to become 'one nation under God.'

Indeed, in many ways the real struggle had only just begun.

A profound change took place in America, and indeed throughout the western world, for the possibilities of democracy seized the imagination of idealists everywhere. In a few years, the French would trigger their own revolution, boasting that, unlike America, their new republic would achieve the Brotherhood of Man, without the Fatherhood of God as a prerequisite. . . . Its proponents made it a new secular religion, and its evangelists, among them American heroes like Tom Paine, brought their faith to our shores with missionary zeal. And because no strong, vital, appealing Christian faith opposed them, almost overnight their cynical, mocking Deism made astonishing inroads into the centers of our creative thinking.

An antispiritual invasion rolled over our land. But as He
always had in the past, God raised up the men to stop it . . .

The North was rapidly becoming an industrialized society,
while the South, with its much greater heat and humidity,
was destined to play an agricultural role, and the West
beckoned small farmers from all other sections.

It appeared, therefore, that God's plan for America,
during the first half century of her independence, was
essentially to preserve the possibility of her fulfilling her call,
while the enemy did all he could to divide her house against
itself prematurely, with slavery his most effective wedge.
—Peter Marshall and David Manuel,
introduction to *From Sea to Shining Sea*[80]

WHAT PRICE FREEDOM!

America was established in the eighteenth century on the principles written in the Declaration of Independence and the Constitution, its most important documents. But it remained for the nineteenth century to shape and form this new land of freedom. In the process, some of the most important events of the nineteenth century proved to be a blessing while some proved to be a curse.

Nothing happens in a moment. The seed of each event in the life of a man or a nation is planted long before its occurrence—often tens or hundreds or thousands of years before. Amazing events had occurred all over the world, culminating in the formation of the United States of America and the adoption of its Constitution. No other nation had ever been founded upon such a great idea—the inalienable rights of its citizens to life, liberty, and the pursuit of happiness.

This nation was established with a unique representative form of government that permitted the citizens to express their will through their elected president and representatives. In no other land were the elected officials so sensitive to the needs and desires of their local electorate; these needs and desires centered around the sovereignty of each state and the people's right to exercise their "inalienable rights" as citizens. The remarkable checks and balances placed in the Constitution by its drafters provided assurance that this representative form of government, with freedom as its cornerstone, would endure the ages. Everything was in place for America to fulfill its destiny as one nation under God.

But freedom is not an event. It is a process. The essence of freedom is centered in the choices made and the consequences of those choices. The choices and how they played out in the history of this nation would determine whether the bells of "freedom" would continue to ring in this land as they rang in Philadelphia in the days of revolution and at the adoption of the Constitution.

The pursuit of liberty and freedom in a nation was not unique to America; Rome and Greece had expressions of liberty and freedom. During the formative years in Rome and Greece, national leaders planted in the hearts of the people a vision of national purpose and a common commitment to that purpose; in exchange, the leaders promised their citizens would have the freedom to carry out those purposes. But freedom requires the yoke of restraint; it must be diligently pursued; freedom is only freedom as long as a nation, its leaders, and its people seek it, both in their lives and as a national expression. When Rome and Greece lost their vision, they lost their united commitment, and their demise was inevitable.

America started with such promise! So had Rome and Greece! But a critical factor distinguished America from its predecessors—in addition to the concepts of freedom and liberty expressed so nobly in America's founding documents, this nation was established through a covenantal relationship with God. For America to develop and flourish as a great nation under God, it not only had to relentlessly guard the "inalienable rights" of its citizens to life, liberty, and the pursuit of happiness, but, more importantly, it had to honor the covenantal relationship with God that brought it into existence. The freedom that was to be this nation's lifeblood came from God through this covenant.

Establishing freedom in a nation presents unique challenges, because freedom means different things to different people. For freedom to endure in a republic, there must be a national consensus that defines and redefines freedom throughout the course of the nation's history. Although the word "freedom" raises as many different ideas as there are people considering it, there is an aspect to true freedom that exists whether people choose to believe in it or not; for freedom to endure, it must be based upon enduring truth.

Jesus said, "You shall know the truth and the truth shall set you free." If these words are true, then any "freedom" not established on the sovereignty of God and the truth of His Word is an illusion. Any act done in the exercise of freedom, but contrary to God's truth, will diminish freedom. God has established rules that define his sovereignty, and any violation of those rules enslaves. True freedom, as the founding fathers were well aware, prevents anarchy, for it is not without restraint; it must be based upon truth and truth's demand that its citizens seek to do that which is right and refrain from doing that which is wrong. There must be limitations on the citizens' opportunity to do whatever they want, and this truth must be written both in the laws of the nation and in the hearts of its citizens. Freedom is the ability to choose the truth. A recognition of God's sovereignty should inevitably lead to a mutual respect for others as children of God and the decision to do that which is right in God's eyes. The great events of the nineteenth century forced this nation and its citizens to choose how the pursuit of freedom (and with it the pursuit of truth) would affect the destiny of this nation. The choices made would determine whether the citizens of this nation would continue to be free.

The struggle to define freedom was to be the great battle of the nineteenth century and was fought on several fronts.

(1) DIVISION AMONG CHURCHES. Because of this covenantal relationship, America began with a special relationship with God demonstrated by its national and church leaders, but forces were already at work that would challenge this Christian heritage. Those who came to this land for the opportunity to worship freely provided the greatest chance

for this to be a Christian nation. The churches they established at the center of all of the great events of the early days of America were the driving force of a nation founded upon the brotherhood of man and the fatherhood of God. Unlike the confrontational churches in Europe, America's churches began with a spirit of cooperation. However, denominational differences began to divide the church, weakening this spirit. Such division diminished the church's ability to influence the national definition of freedom.

(2) HUMANISM AND OTHER RELIGIONS. The idea of freedom based on truth clashed with a humanistic and worldly idea of "freedom" that ignored the covenantal relationship with God and permitted the introduction of every form of religion that could be conceived by the mind of man; this nation as "one nation under God" became a nation under every god. Traces of humanism were evident through the influence of European philosophers in the drafting of the Constitution and more apparent when the ideas espoused during the French Revolution spread across the world.

The twentieth century would see humanism so prevalent that the U.S. Supreme Court gave it a special place in American life formerly reserved for Christianity.

The emergence of humanism and other religions in America is a clear sign that the Church has lost its vision and influence.

(3) THE STRUGGLE TO DEFINE CHRISTIANITY. As a stone dropped in the middle of a calm pool of water causes ripples to the shore, so historical events ripple throughout history even for hundreds or thousands of years. From the time Adam and Eve made their choice in the Garden of Eden,

every nation on the earth has become a battleground between God and Satan. Satan always takes advantage of man's frailties and failures. When Abel, the son of Adam and Eve, brought a blood offering before God, his brother, Cain, brought a grain offering from the fruit of his own labor. God accepted the offering of Abel because it represented submission to God and his divine redemptive plan. But Cain's offering, which represented his attempt to please God by his own efforts, was not accepted. When Cain became angry with God and slew his brother, he set in motion forces that would influence the history of man and this new land called America. Two ways to worship God have reverberated throughout the history of man ever since that fateful event. After the crucifixion of Jesus, there have been, and always will be, the true believers who realize that they have nothing to offer except through the blood offering of the crucified Son; there will also be those who strive to please God by their own efforts, and there will always be jealousy and conflict between the two. In America, before and after the drafting of the Constitution, the spirit of Cain was evident in a large part of the church as it focused on human efforts to please God. Through the powerful ministries of Edwards and Whitefield, this nation and its churches had united together to take a stand for freedom that led to the Revolution and the Constitution; but after the Revolution, the church in America no longer clearly understood, and failed to express, God's redemptive plan for this nation and its citizens.

(4) FEAR OF A CHURCH STATE. Early Americans feared a national church. From the time of Constantine in the fourth century, when the Church was legally recognized by the

Roman Empire, the Church and the State have been the two dominant forces in Europe.[81] The early Americans remembered the oppressive acts of the Church and State in Europe that forced them to travel to America. The founders of the Constitution therefore prohibited the states from establishing a national religion. Although the reasoning behind this prohibition was founded on the desire to keep the people of America free from an oppressive government-run church and able to worship freely, a national concern developed that the Church might have too much influence, which led twentieth century courts to exclude God from every public forum.

(5) STATES' RIGHTS. A struggle in America between national rights and states' rights further weakened the national commitment to freedom. At the time of its revolution, America consisted of thirteen diverse colonies with different interests and a lack of a common commitment. The revolution brought them together in one national expression of freedom; but once freedom was attained, because each colony jealously guarded its own independence, adopting a constitution with a national expression of freedom was extremely difficult. After the Constitution was adopted, the colonies (now states) were reluctant to surrender their local sovereignty. This struggle for states' rights was one of the primary causes of the Civil War and is evident on the political scene today.

(6) INFLUENCE OF THE ENGLISH "REVOLUTION." There were also outside forces influencing America that had a profound effect upon the development of America and its concepts of liberty and freedom.

In the eighteenth century, Great Britain experienced what Charles Dickens referred to as "the best of times, the worst of times." The 1700s produced some of the most powerful tides of revival since Pentecost throughout Great Britain and the emergence of the Industrial Revolution that was to change the British Isles forever. At the same time, Britain's largest church, the Church of England, hand in hand with the state, persecuted all who sought to worship God in any other manner.[82] Even during the Industrial Revolution, the social conditions throughout the British Isles failed to improve; schools were reserved for the wealthy, while the common people lived in poverty; cities were overpopulated; crimes and mob violence prevailed; and infant mortality was high. The poverty and moral degradation that existed at the time have been dramatically portrayed by the writings of Charles Dickens, author of *A Tale of Two Cities* and *Oliver Twist*. Moral laxity was exhibited in the late seventeenth and early eighteenth centuries by English nobility who were notorious for their lives of unfettered licentiousness. The moral depravity of England was challenged by the Puritans, but many of the Puritan leaders were imprisoned because they failed to conform to the "active uniformity." As a result of the Industrial Revolution, England acquired colonies throughout the world to the point that England proudly proclaimed that the sun never set on its flag. At the same time Wesley, Whitefield, and others, ministering in open-air meetings to ten, twenty, or thirty thousand people at a time, gave hope to the people of England, thus averting a revolution similar to the French Revolution. The English "revolution" dramatically influenced America in two ways. First, Englishmen Wesley and Whitefield, ministering throughout America, were to plant the seed for the first great American spiritual awakening.

Second, the imperialistic nature of England planted a similar nature in America that has been evidenced throughout America's history.

(7) INFLUENCE OF THE FRENCH REVOLUTION. The second revolution occurred in France. On July 14, 1789, a small group of Frenchmen captured the old castle-prison called the Bastille. This act of rebellion by the common people originally was a justifiable reaction to a corrupt and manipulative church and the excesses and mistreatment of the common people by the nobility. Although the revolution was initially directed against the crown and nobility, the people's rage was soon aimed at the Roman Catholic Church, and eventually all of Christianity.[83] In order to avoid persecution, nominal Protestants, as well as Roman Catholics, melted into the new infidelity, and an almost universal contempt for all religion occurred.[84] The attack on the Bastille marked not only the downfall of the old church-state in France, but also the emergence of a wholesale rejection of any profession of Christian faith, and the acceptance of the idea that a society may exist without God.[85] On August 27, 1789, the National Assembly of France declared the Rights of Man, based upon the American Declaration of Independence, but without the fatherhood of God. The French Revolution thus birthed the idea of a modern secular state with deep roots in enlightenment and an even deeper resentment of any religious expression.

When the wrath of the French Revolution turned against the Roman Catholic Church, the National Assembly ordered the sale of ecclesiastical lands, closed monasteries and nunneries, and declared freedom of conscience. Bishops and clergy who agreed with principles of the new constitution were elected, and those who did not fled France. The Protestants, as well as the Catholics, quickly turned from their Christian faith. On the eve of the revolution, there were half a million adherents of the Reformed faith in France. By 1793, all of the churches in Paris were closed, and in all of France almost every Protestant church was shut down.[86]

In the third quarter of the eighteenth century this same skepticism made its way to England. England, and later America, were influenced by Thomas Paine, who was in England during the French Revolution; but because of the Wesley and Whitefield influence in England, the excesses of the French Revolution caused a backlash among British working class and aristocracy alike.[87]

Anti-religion, fostered by the French Revolution, spread to Scotland, Ireland, Germany, the Netherlands, Switzerland, Spain, and Portugal. In Spain and Portugal, the militant Society of Jesus was dissolved. In Germany, the revivals gave way to philosophical pursuits.[88] The French Revolution affected all of the countries of western Christendom and produced a more intolerant and defensive Roman Catholic regime which set back the cause of evangelical Christianity. Religious skepticism produced from the French Revolution was to be one of the major challenges for America throughout the nineteenth and twentieth centuries. The moral effects of the Enlightenment led Voltaire, as the French Revolution led Thomas Paine, to predict that Christianity would soon be archaic.[89]

(8) DECLINE OF MORALS AND RELIGION IN AMERICA. The general decline in morals and religion also affected the United States of America. Due to the unsettled state of society

following the Revolutionary War, the breaking up of family and church relationships due to migration, and fierce individualism, America was ripe for social change. The turning away of America from its religious mooring had a profound effect upon the nation in the late eighteenth century. During that period, the United States experienced 300,000 alcohol-abusers; approximately 15,000 were buried annually. Lawlessness, gambling, and slavery dramatically increased. Churchmen were alarmed because the churches were empty. The moral decline extended to all of society, including students in colleges; collegians readily accepted philosophical ideas, which excluded Christianity as a real influence in society.[90] Thomas Dwight, president of Yale, stated that from France, Germany, and Britain, "the dregs of infidelity were vomited upon us . . . the whole mass of pollution was emptied upon this country." Most students at Harvard were atheists; students at Williams College conducted a mock celebration of Holy Communion; and Christians at Princeton were so unpopular that they met in secret.[91] By the end of the eighteenth century, only a few years after the drafting of the Constitution, few college graduates in America professed to be Christians.[92]

(9) AMERICA'S TREATMENT OF ITS INHABITANTS. During the Constitutional Convention, slavery was already an issue; in order to avoid a confrontation about the issue of slavery at the convention, representatives from Virginia claimed that slavery was passing away and would soon end.[93] The slave owners considered their slaves to be "property" that did not have the dignity to be called human. Throughout the next fifty to sixty years, the number of slaves brought from

Africa would dramatically increase while a Northern-based national consensus of the evil of slavery emerged. The slavery issue threatened to tear the nation apart.

Although the early Americans decried freedom, they did not consider that such freedom extended to the Native American Indians. From the time the colonies were established, the history of America, in its dealing with the Native American Indians, is the history of broken promises and treaties, and repeated dispossession of the Native Americans from their home. When the Constitution was written, the rights of the Native Americans did not even merit a comment.

Even though America claimed to be a land of liberty, it did not extend equal opportunity to its citizens, including women. This issue would be a source of conflict in this nation throughout its history.

(10) THE EFFECT OF DEISM IN AMERICA. Deism, which was introduced to America through France and England in the eighteenth century, has dramatically affected this nation. Deism taught that God created the world and turned it over to man to operate. Deists rejected any supernatural religion and denied that the revelation of God came only through the Bible. The doctrine of Deism acknowledged that God created the world, but rejected the idea that God had any active role in the affairs of the world after creation. The Deists argued against the divinity of Jesus Christ and exalted man's reason; anything that was not produced by man's reason, such as the crucifixion of Christ, His resurrection, and all things supernatural, was systematically rejected. In the process Deists sought to disprove all Christian dogmas and biblical miracles, such as a virgin birth. In the late nineteenth century and early

twentieth century, large segments of the church and leading American politicians embraced Deism, denying the supernatural expressions of the Bible and thus diminishing the church's effectiveness.[94] Thomas Jefferson and Thomas Paine were Deists. Paine's book *The Age of Reason,* which espouses Deist philosophy, was widely read in America, particularly in the universities.

But the picture of George Whitefield riding from one end of the colonies and tirelessly preaching two or three sermons a day, and the influence of the Protestant Reformation of the seventeenth century were not forgotten. The church was the driving force for freedom only a few years before; even though it appeared to be sleeping, when awakened, the church could once again define the destiny of this nation.

The man pondered all these things and wondered how a loving God who gave Americans this land of freedom along with the right to choose and determine this nation's destiny could patiently watch America drift from its Christian moorings and turn away from its intended destiny. The man lifted his eyes to the Father and asked, "Father, how can you watch these events occur without intervening? You see what has happened in this land in the last 200 years. This nation has rejected You and Your Son. There was such hope. The bells of freedom were ringing loudly in Philadelphia and throughout the land. This nation was to be a noble experiment—one nation under God."

And the Father answered, "Remember, my son, I rule in the affairs of this nation. I am the one who established this nation as a land of freedom. And what is freedom without the right to choose? And what does it mean to choose to be free without the choice not to be? And what is a choice without the possibilities considered?

"But there is always a risk with any choice. It may be the wrong choice and may play into the hands of the prince of this world. There is an expression, 'Let him give us his best shot.' Remember the story of Job."

Chapter 9

Blow the trumpet in Zion, declare
a holy fast, call a sacred assembly.
Gather the people, consecrate the assembly;
bring together the elders, gather the children,
those nursing at the breast. Let the bridegroom
leave his room and the bride her chamber.
Let the priests, who minister before the Lord,
weep between the temple porch and the altar.
Let them say, 'Spare your people, O Lord.
Do not make your inheritance an object of scorn,
a byword among the nations. Why should they
say among the peoples, 'Where is their God?'
—Joel 2:15–17 NIV

SECOND GREAT AWAKENING

I marveled at the words of the Father. When God created man with a will, mind, and emotion, He created one with whom He could share His love and His plans for planet Earth. But if the relationship with God and man was to be meaningful, man would have to have the right to choose. Except to the extent that man chooses to be obedient to the Father, Satan, the prince of this world, has authority to torment and manipulate. The same is true in the history of nations. The story of Job demonstrates how man had become the object of the great struggle between God and Satan over the destiny of the earth.

One day, the angels of heaven appeared before the Father, and Satan was there. God said, "Consider my servant, Job. There is none like him on all of the earth."

Satan replied, "That is because you have built a hedge around him. Withdraw the hedge, and see what happens."

The Father answered, "Everything he has is yours, but do not harm him."

Satan unleashed his fury against Job, but Job did not waiver in his commitment to the Father.

On another day, the angels appeared before the Father, and Satan was there. The Father said, "Have you considered my servant, Job? There is none like him in all the earth." And Satan replied, "Strike his body, and see what happens."

Using American colloquialism and paraphrasing the Father's response: "Okay, Satan. Give him your best shot, but do not take his life."

After all of Satan's attacks, Job was shaken but not broken. In the end, the Father blessed Job and prospered him twice as much as before.

The earth has been a battleground between God and Satan. And the real battle has been for the mind, will, and spirit of man. The Father may encourage or challenge man or permit circumstances to occur to bring man to a point of decision, but God will never violate man's will. Therefore, even though God's plan will ultimately prevail in the history of the earth and a nation, man will be the instrument through which that plan will be implemented. God always looks for a man or a people to carry out his plan.

The most intense battleground has been for the Jews and the land that God gave to their forefather, Abraham. Because Abraham trusted God like no other man, God called his children a holy nation, a people set apart to Him, and He gave Abraham his land as a land of promise. Since the days of Abraham, God and Satan have waged an ongoing battle for Abraham's land and the mind, will, and spirit of all of his children. God could end that battle at any time, but He will not violate the right of human beings to make their own choices. The primary choice at the center of every battle over Abraham's land is whether Abraham's descendants will give their allegiance to God or to Satan. They must each make that choice. The Father will not make it for them.

There is a second land of promise chosen by the Father. It is a land conceived in liberty and dedicated to the proposition that all citizens of that land may live in freedom. It is the United States of America. God and Satan have battled over this land since before the day Christopher Columbus left Spain by ship heading west. This battle is the essence of freedom, for it is centered in the choices of Americans and the consequences of those choices.

In every battle, each point of conflict becomes a separate battle-ground. Often individual battles appear to result in final defeat or victory. So it has been in America. There has been an ebb and flow in the battle for the soul of this nation. Often it appears that Satan has won; but even though God has given man the right to choose, He rules in the affairs of nations. The last chapters of this nation's history have not yet been written.

After the days in Philadelphia, when our forefathers declared America's independence and wrote its Constitution, the ebb and flow of the battle for the soul of this nation is apparent in its history.

Within a decade after the Constitution was adopted, it appeared to Christians in America that this nation had lost its soul to the philosophies of Europe. America was a wealthy and challenging land. The churches, which were at the center of each village and prominent forces for freedom, had lost their influence, since the primary focus of the Americans was a lust for wealth and land. The pioneers were heading west to new and fertile farmland. There appeared to be no time for God and no place in their lives for religion.

Paine's *Age of Reason* and other works of European philosophy were pervading the universities, and few students professed a belief in the Lord Jesus Christ.

Other forces were at work. In the early 1800s, America was threatened with destruction from internal and external forces. Issues concerning states' rights and the right to own slaves threatened to divide the nation. In newspapers and in the halls of Congress, the word "secession" was repeatedly used as a battle cry. The British military appeared ready to accomplish what it had failed to do in the 1770s. To make matters even worse, it appeared that this new nation had lost its Christian moorings; at the end of the American Revolution, the founders of the Constitution spoke of the providence of the Almighty God; now, following the adoption of a Constitution, there were many in this nation proclaiming that there was no God. Others were questioning whether it mattered if there was a God. At the college of William and Mary, established in the 1700s to give a pious education to Anglicans, students were debating whether Christianity had been helpful or harmful to humanity. Only two students at Princeton professed to be Christians in 1782.[95]

Even though America had just obtained its independence from England, English influence was paramount in America in the late eighteenth century. A spiritual awakening began in England in the 1780s and reached its peak in the 1790s. In northern, southern and western England, there was a noticeable spiritual change and a general revival of religion. John Wesley, a spiritual veteran at the age of eighty-three, journeyed around England in the spring of 1784 and reported an extensive awakening around Newcastle-under-Lyme, saying, "This country is all on fire, and the flame is still spreading from village to village."[96]

Forty years earlier, John Erskine of Edinburgh had published a text enlisting the praying people in Scotland and elsewhere to engage in intercession for the work of the Holy Spirit in all of the churches. His writings were adopted by the Baptists as a "concert of prayer" in 1786. The Baptists were also inspired by the works of Matthew Henry, the famous commentator, who said, "When God intends great mercy for His people, He first of all sets them a-praying."[97]

Revival spread throughout all of England with a common and recurring feature. The move of God was supported by the established churches and prayer societies, but was primarily a spontaneous gathering for prayer; Englishmen responded as great crowds evidenced a mass hunger for something meaningful. Revival also spread to Wales, which was to be the catalyst for the great worldwide revival of the early twentieth century. Before 1800, there was a general awakening throughout Wales, and the movement was "so wholesome, so full of grace and power, and so lasting in effect that the morals of the people were raised to new heights. . . ."[98] Revivals also spread throughout Scotland, Ireland, and the Scandinavian countries.

And then came the second Great Awakening in America.

As in Great Britain, the occasional awakenings occurred locally in the 1780s. These local revivals raised up leaders for the awakening that was to follow. In 1782 in Boscawen, New Hampshire, a pastor of a small inland church identified by J. Edwin Orr only as Dr. Wood, initiated a movement that lasted for twenty years; out of that tiny community came no less than 100 students for college, of whom more than forty entered the Christian ministry. Likewise, in the mid-1780s, a series of awakenings occurred in western Pennsylvania which enlisted Christian leaders for the work that was to follow.[99] Other local awakenings occurred in New England in the 1790s, initiated by the "concert of prayer."

The "concert of prayer," inspired by John Erskine's writings, spread to America. In the 1790s, two Baptist leaders who were influenced by Erskine's text circulated letters in New England calling for prayer for revival. All major denominations supported this call for prayer. A powerful revival touched the First and Second Baptist Churches of Boston, and revivals spread to many congregations in the area. Revivals also spread to Maryland and Delaware.[100]

Presbyterian synods of New York and New Jersey issued a similar call for prayer, followed by the Methodist Episcopal Church, Congregationalists, and the Baptist Association. Throughout the country, the Methodist Episcopal Church dedicated its time to prayer and fasting.[101]

Even more dramatic revivals occurred in Kentucky. Kentucky was a wild, lawless, frontier state. The Kentuckians were reckless, lawless, violent, and brave whiskey drinkers who epitomized the frontier spirit. Of all the untamed territories in America, the settlers in Kentucky were the most isolated, and they considered themselves free and independent.[102]

One of the roughest counties in Kentucky was Logan County, called "Rouges Harbor." Murderers, horse thieves, highway robbers, and counterfeiters fled there in great numbers until they formed a majority and ruled the county.[103] Into Rouges Harbor in 1798 came a preacher, James McGready, who established three congregations located on the Muddy, the Red, and the Gasper rivers in Logan County. In each settlement his first appeal was a covenant to pray for revival. Those who were willing to sign the covenant committed themselves to pray every Saturday evening and Sunday morning and to devote the third Saturday of each month to prayer and fasting. Revival tarried and it seemed that things were worse, but McGready and his prayers continued. Then, within a year, revival began to break out. At Red River in 1799 at the quarterly communion services, "some of the boldest, most daring sinners in the county covered their faces and wept bitterly."[104] The celebration of the Lord's Supper at Gasper River Church saw similar results.

In June of 1800 at the quarterly communion service at the Red River Church, more than 500 showed up, with some having traveled more than 100 miles. The meeting lasted four days, and at the final meeting on the last day, the power of God fell. A solemn weeping descended on the crowd. During that meeting, the dam broke, the flood of salvation swept through the assembly, and the floor was "covered with the slain; their screams for mercy pierced the heavens."[105]

From there, McGready went to Muddy River with similar results. In July of 1800, he moved to Gasper River Church for a four-day sacrament meeting that 10,000 people attended, which was astonishing since Logan County was in the backwoods, and the nearest town, Lexington, with a population of 1,800 inhabitants, was more than one hundred miles away. McGready invited other backwoods ministers to join him. The power of God fell on this crowd as it had at the earlier meetings.[106]

Barton Stone, a Presbyterian minister, described this meeting:

> The scene was new to me and passing strange. It baffled description. Many, very many, fell down as men slain in battle and continued for hours together in an apparently breathless and motionless state, sometimes for a few minutes reviving and exhibiting symptoms of life by a deep groan or a piercing shriek, or by a prayer for mercy, fervently uttered. After lying there for hours, they obtained deliverance. The gloomy cloud that had covered their faces seemed gradually and visibly to disappear, and hope in smiles brightened into joy. They would rise shouting deliverance, and then would address the surrounding multitudes in language truly eloquent and impressive. With astonishment did I hear men, women, and children declaring the wonderful works of God and the glorious mysteries of the Gospel.[107]

Barton Stone returned from Logan County to his home in Bourbon County intent on holding a similar meeting in his county. He immediately began to plan a meeting at Cane Ridge the following summer. For days before the meeting was to commence, the roads were crowded with wagons, carriages, horses, and men on foot proceeding to the camp meeting. To everyone's amazement, more than 25,000 people showed up, representing more than one-eighth of the state's free population. During the four-day meeting, the power of God fell in dramatic ways on those in attendance.[108]

J. Edwin Orr, in *The Eager Feet,* reported the following:

Quite a number of people suffered prostration, that is, physical collapse, generally remaining conscious but helpless. Much more frightening, subjects of conviction began to tremble, the trembling giving way to spasmodic jerking. This reaction appeared in people who resisted the message or ridiculed it, as well as in willing hearers. Scoffers came armed with pricks and prods and bottles of whiskey to keep themselves from falling under the influence, to no avail—then their fright became alarming. People helpless under this influence wailed or groaned or cursed or struggled.[109]

In the weeks and months following, revival broke out in church after church, camp meeting after camp meeting, and a chain reaction began in county after county in Kentucky and Tennessee. By January of 1801, the awakening had reached Nashville and Knoxville, Louisville and Lexington. The awakening had a profound effect on all of Kentucky. Dr. George A. Baxter reported his travels throughout Kentucky:

On my way, I was informed by settlers on the road that the character of Kentucky was entirely changed, and that they were as remarkable for sobriety as they had formerly been for dissoluteness and immorality. And indeed I found Kentucky to appearances the most moral place I have ever seen. A profane expression was hardly ever heard. A religious awe seemed to pervade the country. Upon the whole, I think that the revival in Kentucky the most extraordinary that has ever visited the Church of Christ.[110]

The concert of prayer enlisted many intercessors in the southern states. In Virginia, North Carolina, South Carolina, Georgia, and the Mississippi Territory, the Anglicans, Baptists, Methodists, Presbyterians, and other denominations were engaged in prayer. Even before the extraordinary movement in Kentucky, a revival occurred in the Rocky River Presbyterian Church in North Carolina in 1798 that was so lasting in its effects that ten years later a day of thanksgiving for the work was celebrated with enthusiasm. When news of the outpouring of the Spirit in Kentucky and Tennessee began to reach the western part of North Carolina, revival swept a gathering for communion at Cross Roads in 1801. Two hundred sixty-two wagonloads of people descended upon Cross Roads, bringing the attendance of the communion service to 10,000 people. The awakening in North Carolina attracted huge crowds across the state from 1802 through 1805. The vast crowds gathered in open fields, and ministers of all denominations assisted.[111]

In South Carolina, 3,500 people attended a service in Lexington County. This meeting was described by Orr as follows:

As the gathering met in the open field, and not in a local church, a host of scoffers assembled with them to mock at the proceedings. It was chiefly among these antagonists that physical prostrations occurred. Loud-mouthed and defiant critics collapsed in a heap. Some, seeing what was happening, came fortified by strong drink, even waving their bottles, but went down like ninepins, wailing in fear. One such scoffer was smitten to the ground. When at last some concerned minister got round to him, he urged the helpless man lying prostrate on the ground to pray. 'I'll be damned if I do,' the sinner panted. He lay helpless all night, and was last seen creeping away on all fours. Some sinners fell instantaneously, as if struck by lightning, and lay helpless but conscious, full of apprehension and conviction.[112]

Revival spread to Georgia. In July 1802 Moses Waddel attended a four-day meeting at a little Presbyterian church named Nazareth, and was startled by "persons falling to the ground as suddenly as if they had been pierced through the heart by a bullet or a sword." The number attending was estimated from 5,000 to 8,000 people. Throughout 1802 camp meetings continued, with one meeting attracting 10,000, ministered to by twenty-five pastors of various denominations.[113]

It was on the college campuses that the European philosophies of Skepticism, Deism, and Atheism had taken root in this nation through the writings of Voltaire, Rousseau, and others. Now these campuses were transformed by the second Great Awakening.[114]

The first college to experience revival was Hampden-Sydney in Virginia. In 1787, four Christian students met in a forest away from the campus to pray. They were discovered by the other students and ridiculed as fanatics. A near riot ensued. The president of the college, John Brown Smith, who was converted in the first Great Awakening, invited the four students to meet with him. Revival broke out and one-half of the student body was affected. Soon revival spread to nearby counties. The college was visited by revival periodically for the next three decades.[115]

Revival also broke out in Yale College. Timothy Dwight became president in 1795. The spiritual condition of the college was deplorable, and most students espoused the philosophies of Voltaire and Rousseau. Dwight began to teach the Bible as the Word of God. Changes were gradual, but in 1802, when two students publicly professed their faith in Jesus Christ, dozens followed. By the end of the year, one-half of the students were converted, and nearly one-third entered the ministry.[116]

At Williams College in Massachusetts, a group of students was meeting for prayer on a warm August day in 1806. A rainstorm drove them to the shelter of a haystack, where they continued to pray in what is called the "Haystack Revival." While there, one of their members proposed a mission project to India. Out of that meeting came the first foreign mission organization in America.[117]

Revivals often are short-lived, but this revival lasted more than fifty years. The impetus and sustaining power of the second Great Awakening came from the Methodist circuit-riding preachers who followed in the footsteps of George Whitefield, the primary ministering force of the first Great Awakening. The Methodist circuit riders traveled on their horses at all hours of the day or night in good weather and bad, always headed to the next house or settlement to spread the good news of Christ. More than one-half of the Methodist circuit riders of that day died before their thirty-third birthday. One traveler said he had never been to a house in Kentucky that had not been visited by a Methodist preacher.[118]

The two best-known circuit riders were Francis Asbury and Peter Cartwright. All of the frontier was Asbury's parish. He rode by horseback from 4,000 to 6,000 miles per year. During his forty-five years of labor in America, he wore out three horses, and finally in later years took to riding in carts. He preached wherever his horse stopped.[119]

Cartwright was a powerful man and known as a "two-fisted preacher." He traveled the backwoods of Kentucky. In the sparsely settled Kentucky he claimed that 10,000 souls came to the Lord under his ministry, and 20,000 were received into the church.[120]

The final impetus of the second Great Awakening was furnished by Charles Finney, a lawyer who had little interest in religion.

When he started attending a church and became its music director, a group of young people began to pray for his conversion, one of whom was later to become his wife. He started to read the Bible, and finally set a date to settle the issue of his own salvation. He spent that day alone in prayer, and at the end of the day "the Holy Spirit descended upon me in a manner that seemed to go through me, body and soul."[121]

Wherever Finney went, revival followed. On one occasion, in a hotel where he was staying, a group of travelers was overwhelmed by the power of God.[122] In Utica, New York, while he toured a factory, workers began to fall under conviction. The power of God was so great that the factory manager stopped work to let the workers "attend to religion."[123]

Under Finney's ministry in Rochester, New York, in 1831, approximately one-tenth of the city's population came to Christ, and the moral atmosphere of the city was greatly changed. Similar results followed in other cities in New York and Rhode Island. It is said that his ministry led to the salvation of 500,000 people, but the primary effect of his ministry was the emphasis it placed on the transformation of society by the Spirit of Christ. His writings, which are in general circulation today, have fueled many revivals, and led others to commit their lives to pray for the transformation of the social condition of man.[124]

The second Great Awakening (sometimes referred to as the second and third Great Awakenings) dramatically changed American life. This awakening, which started in 1792, ran for fifty years, after which followed a decline; but after a fifteen-year period of decline, there came another Great Awakening, which surpassed the previous movements in its extent, wholesomeness, effect, and lasting impact.[125]

The man pondered the events of the second Great Awakening. When it appeared that Christianity had lost its position as the driving force of American society, God visited this nation with revival. And through the sacrifices of the circuit-riding preachers, that revival reached all of the nation, including its new frontiers.

The man lifted his eyes to the Father and said, "I marvel at how quickly things can change. When it appears that the whole nation has turned away from you, revival comes, and the spiritual climate of the nation changes."

And the Father replied, "Remember, I look for a man to build up the walls and stand in the gap before me on behalf of the land. Often there is none, but sometimes there is one. You see what I can do when there are those truly committed to me.

"Continue your journey to see what I will reveal."

Chapter 10

The Winchester Republican *newspaper
described Chief Justice John Marshall's appearance
at a local tavern after he encountered trouble
with his carriage along the road:*

*"In the tavern a discussion arose among some
young men concerning 'the merits of the
Christian religion.' The debate grew warm and
lasted 'from six o'clock until eleven.' No one
knew Marshall, who sat quietly listening.*

*Finally, one of the youthful combatants
turned to him and said: 'Well, my old
gentleman, what think you of these things?'*

*Marshall responded with a 'most eloquent
and unanswerable appeal.' He talked for an hour,
answering 'every argument urged against' the
teachings of Jesus. 'In the whole lecture, there
was so much simplicity and energy, pathos and
sublimity, that not another word was uttered.'*

*The listeners wondered who the old man
could be. Some thought him a preacher; and great
was their surprise when they learned afterwards
that he was the Chief Justice of the United States."* [126]

THE BLESSINGS AND THE CURSES

In the history of every nation there are persistent issues that must be addressed. How the nation responds to those issues determines its destiny. Three struggles in the early nineteenth century epitomized America's pursuit of freedom. The way our nation responded in each of these issues produced both a blessing and a curse.

The first involved the rule of law and took place between President Jefferson, Congress, and Chief Justice John Marshall. In their wisdom, the drafters of the Constitution established the Supreme Court as the final arbitrator of the Constitution. Under the tenure of Marshall the role of the courts was to be determined. In the early nineteenth century that role would be severely tested in the confrontation between Jefferson and Madison in the Supreme Court case of *Marbury v. Madison.*

The second issue that was to be a persistent struggle in America was America's treatment of its inhabitants. Less than one hundred years before, Americans had fought and died to establish a nation founded upon the inalienable rights of its citizens to life, liberty, and the pursuit of happiness. In the early nineteenth century, America's visible struggle over individual rights was its struggle with slavery. The great spiritual awakenings of the late eighteenth century and nineteenth century produced a moral consensus in the North that slavery was no longer tolerable. The slavery issue erupted in the early nineteenth century when Congress considered admission of new states and whether such states would be admitted as slave states or free. This struggle was the focal point in America's Civil War when slavery forever ended in this nation. But there were undercurrents of inequality and mistreatment of its inhabitants that would continue to plague America throughout its history.

The third great struggle was epitomized in the early nineteenth century by the War of 1812; through its victory over Great Britain, America survived as a nation and an international power. But America's participation in other wars was to be a blessing and a curse upon this land.

MARSHALL AND THE SUPREME COURT

In the 1800 election, President John Adams, the last Federalist, was voted out of office and replaced by Thomas Jefferson. Because Jefferson was an acknowledged Deist and influenced by European philosophers, committed Christians of the Federalist Party viewed his administration with contempt.[127] As one of his last acts as president, Adams appointed John Marshall chief justice of the United States Supreme Court.

Justice Marshall was well prepared for his role. He had served his nation as deputy judge advocate and demonstrated a rare ability to analyze cases, which was to be his hallmark as chief justice. He was also well respected for his service as a lieutenant under Washington during the difficult days at Valley Forge. Marshall watched the soldiers march into Valley Forge barefoot, leaving bloody tracks behind them in the snow. There he gave his men the clothes that he owned except those that he was wearing. He also observed how often supply wagons never reached the camp and how it was difficult to wage war without a strong central government. From this experience, Marshall concluded that the federal government must have the power to tax, establish laws for the preservation of the nation, and supply an army. Marshall was a Christian; from his study of the life of Jesus and the writings of Paul, he recognized the fallen nature of mankind. Since man was born of a sinful nature, for his own protection he must be under law, and the government must not be manipulated by popular opinion that can shift as quickly as the wind.[128] Marshall had read

Edward Burke's *Reflecting on the Revolution in France,* and he realized that the mass of people must be distrusted when they are an unfettered political force. His service under Washington at Valley Forge and devotion to Christian concepts of the nature of man were to shape the court during Marshall's years of his service as chief justice.

President Jefferson considered the voice of the people to be his mandate; when the people made their will known through elections, the elected officials must carry out the will of the voters.

In the early days of the Marshall court, the Supreme Court met in a cramped basement room in the Capitol, which revealed the lack of respect the legislators had for the highest court of the land.[129] This was to change under Marshall's court.

The battle lines were drawn between Marshall and President Jefferson in the case of *Marbury v. Madison.* During John Adams's last days as president, he appointed a number of justices of the peace for the District of Columbia. When Jefferson became president, he stopped the appointments that were not completed. Marbury, one of the appointees whose commission was stopped, sued Jefferson's secretary of state, James Madison, to recover his commission. The appointments of justices of the peace were made by Adams under laws established by the legislature. To Jefferson the will of the people mandated the cancellation of such appointments. In Marshall's view, Adams's appointments were made under legislative decrees, and any action of the president or the Congress in annulling such appointments must be judged by the Constitution. Marshall realized that the court must be the arbitrator of a law's constitutionality in order to prevent the legislature from making laws and the president from carrying out or changing laws contrary to America's Constitution. Unless the Supreme Court took seriously its role as sole final arbitrator of a law's constitutionality, the Constitution would soon have no effect.

Jefferson's Democratic Republicans showed their contempt for the Supreme Court by closing down the courts and delaying the *Marbury v. Madison* decision for more than a year. Jefferson's party also repealed the Judiciary Act of 1801, thus voiding many of the judicial appointments of Adams at the end of his presidency. To make matters worse, when the Supreme Court reconvened in 1803, the House of Representatives was in the process of impeaching John Pickering, one of Adams's district judge appointees, for "high crimes and misde-meanors." The Democratic Republicans vowed that Supreme Court Justice Samuel Chase would be next because he conducted his court in a partisan manner. Had they been successful in removing Chase, their next target undoubtedly would have been Chief Justice Marshall.

In *Marbury v. Madison,* Marshall and the Supreme Court ruled that the cancellation of Adams's appointments violated the Constitution and was unenforceable. Marshall's court declared that the judiciary could annul a presidential or congressional act that violated the Constitution. Marshall recognized the Constitution as the highest law of the land, and maintained that any attempt on the part of the people or their elected officials to limit its provisions must be rendered void. The Democratic Republican legislators retaliated by seeking to impeach Samuel Chase and thereby remove him from the Supreme Court. When the impeachment proceedings reached the U.S. Senate, John Quincy Adams, with enough other senators to consti-tute a majority, voted "not guilty" and prevented the impeachment, thus preserving the Constitution and vindicating the Supreme Court's decision in *Marbury v. Madison.*[130]

The Marshall court also laid the foundation for a strong central government that could define the rules for commerce between the states. Paul Johnson, in *A History of the American People,* recounted Marshall's belief that it was "the duty of the court so to interpret the

Constitution that the rights of property of all kinds were properly acknowledged, and capitalism thus enabled to do its job of developing the vast territories which Almighty God, in His wisdom, had given the American people just as He had once given the Promised Land to the Israelites."[131] Rulings of Marshall's Supreme Court established and defined the constitutional authority of a strong federal government. In *Fletcher v. Peck,* the Supreme court recognized the validity of a contract even though ordinary men might question whether it is ethical. In *Dartmouth College v. Woodward,* the court ruled that a corporate charter of a private company involved in interstate commerce could not be set aside by a state. In *Gibbons v. Ogden,* the court ruled that a state legislature could not create a steamboat monopoly involved in interstate commerce. In *McCulloch v. Maryland,* the court recognized the right of the federal government to establish a federal bank that the states could not tax[132] in an opinion by Chief Justice Marshall that has been referred to as "perhaps the most celebrated judicial utterance in the annals of the English speaking world."[133]

Without Chief Justice John Marshall and his dedication to the preservation of the Constitution, the rule of law in America would be entirely different; a president acting in unfettered authority could ultimately assert dictatorial power; or a congress could express the impulsive will of the populace, thereby destroying the cause of freedom in this land. If this were to happen, the Constitution, which now preserves the causes of freedom, would lose its preserving power.

Since the days of the Marshall court, the president, Congress, and the American citizens have respected the right of the Supreme Court as the final arbitrator of the law. But neither Marshall nor Jefferson envisioned the day that the United States Supreme Court, often without historical precedence, would use its authority not to interpret the Constitution but to make laws. Marshall, who believed that Almighty God had given the American people this great nation as a new promised land, would be shocked to see the great "wall of separation" between church and state that has been written into the United States Constitution by the Supreme Court in recent years. In the early part of the twentieth century the Supreme Court recognized that America is a Christian nation, acknowledging with reverence a duty of obedience to the will of God *(United States v. Macintosh)*. Then, in *Everson v. Board of Education,* in 1947, the court declared a "wall of separation" between church and state. The Supreme Court has swept aside, one after another, every vestige of Christianity in the schools, assemblies, and public squares. The court's declaration of a separation of church and state has been echoed in classrooms and assembly places throughout the nation, where American citizens have followed the lead of the Supreme Court in rejecting biblical truths and any duty of obedience to the will of God.

Therefore, the history of the Supreme Court, starting with Marshall's court, has been both a blessing and a curse—a blessing in that the Supreme Court has placed restraints on the other branches of government in a proper exercise of the balance of power, but a curse during the twentieth century with abuses of power as acts of political expedience by arrogant justices appointed for life.

MISSOURI AND SLAVERY

During the eighteenth and nineteenth centuries, the states of the union jealously guarded their own state rights; often, this threatened the preservation of the nation. In the halls of Congress, the right of a state to secede was invoked by legislators in moments of anger or frustration. The issues of states' rights threatened national unity when the U.S. Congress sought to admit Missouri as a state. In 1819, Missouri reached the 60,000 population mark, the threshold for admission as a state. Missouri had 10,000 slaves and was acquiring more, and applied for statehood with no restrictions on slavery.[134] There were then eleven slave states and eleven free states.[135]

Congressman James Tallmadge, Jr. of New York proposed an amendment to Missouri's application, which would prevent the acquisition of additional slaves, and free existing slaves.[136] With this amendment, the battle lines were drawn. The South threatened secession if the amendment was adopted, and Tallmadge and others from the North threatened secession if it was not. Marshall and Manuel, in their book *From Sea to Shining Sea,* dramatically describe the political climate that existed in 1819 when Congress met to determine whether Missouri would be admitted to the Union as a slave state. I have paraphrased their story as follows:

While the House of Representatives was debating the issue, parading before the Capitol was a small column of six black male slaves chained together at the waist and neck; following behind them were four scantily dressed females joined together by rope halters around their necks, and four children who were not tethered but followed obediently. The slaves were led by a black driver. Following them on horseback came the white slave trader, with a pistol protruding from his belt and a loosely coiled blacksnake whip in his right hand.

Slowly this small group of slaves passed under the watchful eyes of the congressmen taking air during a recess. They were also watched by the ladies of Washington who were attending the House debate over the Missouri question, the most hotly contested issue in the history of the House of Representatives. The women averted their eyes to avoid the scandalous sight of the thinly clad black women.

Some of the men chuckled and made low observations among themselves, while others turned away. To other men this scene was permanently etched in their memories.

After watching the slaves parade before the Capitol, the congressmen returned to the House of Representatives and addressed the Missouri questions with even greater intensity. Throughout the halls of Congress, legislators cried for an end to slavery. Phrases such as "civil war" and "division" rang throughout the House. Since they were unable to resolve the issue, the House of Representatives recessed for the summer and for the fall elections, but the Missouri question had not been resolved, and the passion of the issue did not subside.

When the House of Representatives reassembled, the slavery issue was settled for the moment through the artful negotiation of Henry Clay, speaker of the House. Clay negotiated a settlement in which the North agreed to admit Missouri as a slave state, and the South withdrew its refusal to admit Maine to the Union as a free state. In addition, the North accepted slavery as far north as Missouri's northern border, while the South agreed that slavery could be excluded north of Missouri.[137]

With the Missouri Compromise, America survived a confrontation that could have resulted in a civil war or permanently torn this young nation apart. Less than fifty years later, this nation went through and survived an agonizing Civil War and came out of that war more united than it had ever been through the visionary proclamations of America's great prophet, Abraham Lincoln, and the commitment to the preservation of the nation by the Southern general, Robert E. Lee. Without these two great men it is likely the nation would have been torn apart by its great Civil War.

The Missouri Compromise was only one of many battles for individual freedom that this nation was to experience. In its treatment of its inhabitants, America has been a paradox. On one hand, this nation has extended its arms to welcome newcomers from all over the world, and millions legally or illegally poured into America each year. At the same time, there are groups of American inhabitants that have not received equal treatment under the law and in the marketplaces of America—blacks, Native American Indians, Hispanics, other minority groups, and even women.

Despite our proclamation that all men are endowed with certain "inalienable rights," America brought millions of blacks from Africa as slaves and then fought an agonizing Civil War to end slavery. When the war ended, Southerners continued to treat blacks with contempt, while Northerners, content that the war was over, looked the other way. The struggle of the blacks for equality continues to this day.

In the drafting of our Constitution and all of its amendments, the Native American Indians were never even mentioned. During the settlement days of this nation, America killed or swept aside and disenfranchised millions of Native American Indians. Their treatment throughout the formative days of this nation and continuing in the nineteenth and twentieth centuries is one of America's great sins. The Native American Indians were particularly vulnerable to mistreatment because they understood the meaning of "covenant" better than those who encroached on their territory; they believed a man's word was his bond and watched as one covenant after another was broken by these new Americans.

In its treatment of women, America followed the lead of Greece and Rome, who virtually disenfranchised women. It often surprises us to remember that women only received the right to vote in 1920. Before that date America had developed a governmental, and business, elite white male class.

Throughout the nineteenth and twentieth centuries, equal opportunity under the law in employment and other areas has not extended to these three groups or to Hispanics and other minority groups, and a great disparity has existed between the earning power of white male American citizens, and women and members of other ethnic groups.

WAR OF 1812

The survival of America was also threatened by external forces when this nation was forced to fight against Britain in the War of 1812. In 1775 the population of America was 3,000,000. By 1800 it had increased to 5,300,000, compared with a population of Great Britain and Ireland totaling 15,000,000. At this rate of growth, the United States population would soon surpass that of its mother country.[138] Nevertheless, Great Britain looked upon America as an upstart nation and treated it with contempt. In the early 1800s, Napoleon and England were at war as Napoleon sought to extend his dominion to Great Britain. Britain maintained a massive naval fleet, but its ships were undermanned, and there were many desertions. In order to man its ships, the British stopped American ships at sea, claiming that the sailors who did not speak like "Yankees" were deserters and forcing them to serve in the British navy.[139]

President Madison's representatives protested, but the British would not consider any change of policy or make atonement for such practices unless the United States agreed to stop trade with Napoleon. At the same time, Britain informed the United States that it would seize any ships that traded with any country under Napoleon's dominion.[140]

Napoleon joined in the game by seizing American vessels in French ports and confiscating their cargo. Thus the new nation was caught in the middle of Britain's war with Napoleon. Because trade was essential for America's economy, Madison's representatives sought to negotiate trade treaties with France; but this only compounded the problem. By the summer of 1812, more than 6,000 American citizens had been kidnapped and forced to serve in the British navy.[141] In a further act of disdain, the British fleet blockaded American ports to prevent ships from exporting American goods. If America was to retain any honor, it must fight, and President Madison declared a state of war. Thus the War of 1812 began.

The naval fleet of the United States was small and ill-prepared for a war with a strong naval power like Great Britain. Jefferson opposed military preparedness. Therefore, no navy or army had been formed since the Revolutionary days. By 1807, there were only ten American ships on active duty.[142]

Fortunately, because of its life-or-death struggle with Napoleon, Great Britain could only give limited attention to its conflict with America. In the early part of the war, America suffered major defeats. American troops fought the British in Canada but were soundly defeated. In sea battles America had some early victories. But in the winter of 1813–1814, when the war with France was winding down, the British Navy concentrated its forces on America and appeared to be in control of its coasts. America's problems were multiplied by its economic weakness. New England states, resentful of America's position in the war, refused to provide financial support.[143] The combination of Jefferson's embargo on trade with Britain and France and British blockades led to the near-bankruptcy of the American economy. New England traded extensively with Great Britain and opposed Jefferson's embargo. Northern states threatened to secede from the Union if war was declared against Britain. The South favored trade with France and insisted on war against England.

In the West, there were threats of secession because the Jefferson and Madison administrations were not giving necessary support in the fight against the Native American Indians.[144]

In August 1814 the British put troops ashore near the nation's capital and marched into Washington while the president hid in the woods nearby.[145] The British torched the capital and ransacked the White House. The next day, when the British undertook to complete the destruction of the American capital, a tornado struck with such force that General Ross, the British general, withdrew his troops from the city. The United States capital was saved by this "act of God."

With 12,000 troops assembled the British set their sights on Baltimore and its major fort, named McHenry, which commanded the entrance to Baltimore's harbor. In addition to the ground forces, the British navy, positioned outside of the harbor, bombarded Fort McHenry with all of its awesome firepower. In all, there were thirty-five British warships and five of the Royal Navy's "boom vessels," which were considered to be the world's greatest naval military ships.

Standing in the way of the British forces was the untested American militia in much smaller numbers and Fort McHenry, flying the largest American flag ever seen. Mary Pickersgill, at the request of the fort commander, had prepared a flag measuring 29 feet by 36 feet to fly over Fort McHenry.

At dawn on Tuesday, September 12, 1814, the British navy unleashed its furious firepower on Fort McHenry. Throughout the day, the British navy bombarded the fort. Finally the British Vice Admiral Cochrane, convinced that Fort McHenry was disabled, sent the British ships in closer. Suddenly the American gunners in the fort responded with fire. One after another of the British ships were hit. Stunned at the response, Cochrane signaled the British bomb ships to withdraw.

Meanwhile on land, the British land forces began to march on Fort McHenry, but the out-manned American militia, with carefully prepared earthworks and superb marksmanship, withstood the British forces.

The British devised a coordinated night attack on Fort McHenry with massive ground forces and naval bombardment. However, Cochrane was not willing to send his fleet close to the shore, and he chose an amphibious assault on the fort accompanied by ground attack and more distant naval bombardment. The plan was put in effect, but another "act of God" occurred—it began to rain heavily. The rain obstructed the vision of the British land forces, who made a wrong turn and marched away from the battlefield. The rain also soaked the firelocks of the British infantry when it did engage in battle, diminishing its effectiveness. Worse for the British, their amphibious forces were spotted before they reached shore. The fort batteries opened fire, and the landing force was compelled to return to its ship.

Cochrane's only choice was to bombard Fort McHenry throughout the night in hopes that the fort would be subdued or destroyed; but during the night, another storm came up. Two Americans were on a British ship under a flag of truce. One was Francis Scott Key, who looked at Fort McHenry and saw Mary Pickersgill's flag still standing by "the rocket's red glare" and the "bombs bursting in air." During that night, as he saw "that our flag was still there," he penned the song that later became America's national anthem. The battle ended, and the British slunk away in defeat. Fort McHenry had withstood what Marshall and Manuel call "the greatest bombardment in naval history."[146]

Another miracle took place on Lake Champlain outside Plattsburg two days before the bombardment of Fort McHenry. The

British prepared to attack with a cavalry of 18,000 men with heavy artillery against a 3,300-man American militia with only one professional battalion. The Americans had four brigs, eight gunboats, and land forces located in the Plattsburg bay. Leaving nothing to chance, the British commander dispatched a large fleet of military sailing ships into the harbor to dispose of the American ships. When they entered the bay, the wind died, leaving the British sail fleet gliding helplessly the full length of the American battle lines; the outcome of the battle was thus decided. The British ships were disabled, and the general leading the land forces became so disheartened that he withdrew his troops. The invasion was over. To add insult to injury, 800 of the British were so disgusted with their general's action that they deserted to the American side.[147]

Both sides were losing heart for battle; but at the same time, other British were approaching the Mississippi Delta to take New Orleans. A victory at New Orleans would give the British access to all of the Mississippi River and an entrance into the virtually indefensible backside of America. The one man who was in a position to resist this attack was "Old Hickory," Andrew Jackson. Jackson, with his Tennessee volunteers, moved to New Orleans, while other volunteers came from Kentucky. When the decisive battle took place, the British numbered 8,000 troops, known as the "Invincibles" because of their outstanding military record, to Jackson's 4,000; but these American volunteers were probably the best marksmen in the world, having learned their trade hunting in the backwoods of Tennessee and Kentucky and in their fights with Native Americans. To the amazement of the British, the American riflemen began picking off British troops some 300 yards away, first shooting the officers.

Using their traditional method of battle, the British troops marched toward the American lines with fixed bayonets. The

Americans were amazed that the British did not fire a shot, but kept coming while the volunteers continued to fire. When one Brit fell, another filled his place. During the battle, the volunteers shot each man they recognized as an officer from long range.

In a rage, British General Gibbs, the only field-grade officer still alive, rode his horse toward the American lines. Four bullets brought him down. With no leader, the assault was finished. The British suffered 1,971 casualties, while the American losses numbered seven killed and six wounded.[148]

The war was over. At last the Americans gained the respect of the British. Never again would America have to defend itself against the British. From that day forward the British and Americans have been political and military allies in every common international encounter.

The War of 1812 was only one of many wars that would engage this nation. Perhaps America's wars more than anything else have demonstrated a covenant relationship between God and this nation. This is true for three reasons: (1) wars have brought loyal Americans to a greater commitment to the cause of freedom; 2) American wars have generally produced a concert of prayer for our nation and its armed forces and; (3) when a nation prays, God hears its prayers.

It is apparent to me from our experiences in prior wars that America is a covenant nation as follows:

(1) Had it not been for God's intervention in the War of Independence and the War of 1812, America never would have gained its independence or continued as a nation. In both of these wars, America was out-manned, but God miraculously intervened at strategic moments to bring about victory or to prevent defeat. In the end it must be said that America was victorious in both of these wars because of the sovereignty of God.

(2) Soon after the War of 1812, America defeated the Mexicans in the Mexican War and extended its borders from the east to the west coast. While America proclaimed its "manifest destiny" to extend from sea to sea, it proved that it was an imperialistic nation ready to seize opportunities to foster its expansion or growth, thus demonstrating America's two natures—one like the soaring eagle, transcending all other nations, and the other like the hawk that devours its prey.

(3) The Civil War was waged and, tragically, hundreds of thousands of America's finest were killed in the battle between brothers. But out of the great Civil War, due to the leadership of Lincoln and Lee, this nation united as one nation more than ever before. In this great struggle Lincoln proclaimed, on behalf of all Americans, this nation's covenant with God.

(4) In World War I, President Wilson and Christian leaders expressed a divine obligation to intervene in a war on a foreign continent, for the preservation of Europe, America and the rest of the world. In World War II, the entire nation mobilized in a war effort that is referred to by Paul Johnson as a "miracle of production." In the process, America became a great military power and proved to the world what it could accomplish through the united efforts of its citizens and the hand of God. Without the intervention of America in these great world wars and America's effort to restore the war-torn land through the Marshall Plan, the world would be much different today.

(5) Then the Cold War was waged for approximately fifty years—not with swords, but with words—until the fall of Communism in the 1990s. The fall of Communism demonstrated to all of the world the depravity of a totalitarian society that seeks to eradicate every vestige of Godly influence.

(6) Mid–twentieth century English historian Arnold Toynbee, in his masterful *Study of History*, concluded that a nation grows at its optimum point of challenge. He used as examples the development of America in the Northeast, which was this nation's greatest point of challenge, and the failure of Caribbean and South Sea islands to develop where life is so easy. He also concluded that a nation that fights wars on foreign soil drains its national strength and resources, because the foreign battlefields become the point of optimum challenge. Toynbee's words proved to be true in the Korean War and Vietnam War when America, without vision, without purpose, and without any clearly defined goals, fought wars that ended in humiliation and virtual defeat, draining America's financial strength. The Vietnam and Korean wars were also fought at a time when America was at a low ebb spiritually, and the wars were not supported by prayers. They differed from World Wars I and II, when the American citizens were properly united and also mobilized in the "miracle of production."

(7) The recent Gulf War demonstrated both the spiritual awakening that is occurring in this land and God's covenantal relationship with this nation. Before entering Kuwait, our forces were told to prepare for thousands of casualties; tens of thousands of body bags were brought to the front. As Americans watched by television while our forces prepared to enter Kuwait, American churches were filled with Christians praying and with yellow ribbons hanging on trees, symbolizing support for our soldiers. A friend who was a lieutenant on the front lines told us, "You don't realize how miraculous this war was." Then he described the tremendous winds that blew with such force before our forces entered Kuwait that the land mines

along the border were exposed; our forces were able to maneuver around the mines without any casualties. Another man who was a sergeant told us, "When scuds landed in Kuwait, strong winds blew from behind the American forces, blowing away any poisonous gas that might have been in the scuds." He added, "There were whirlwinds like the whirlwinds described in the Old Testament." Had it not been for God's divine intervention, thousands of American lives would have been lost in Kuwait. But God heard the prayers of Americans and interceded on behalf of our armed forces.

At the time of this writing, the United States, Great Britain, Australia, and other coalition forces just completed the war in Iraq—a war that has stirred opposition from all Arab countries and prompted threats of terrorist attacks. It remains to be seen: (1) whether America will be victorious in its battle against terrorism; (2) what the worldwide implications of this war will be; and (3) whether Americans will pray in a concert of prayer with the same fervor that they prayed at the time of the Gulf War. America's young men and women, who predominantly joined our armed services to get a college education, are now thrust into the midst of battle against terrorism. Shocked by the atrocities of Saddam Hussein's regime, realizing what it means to live in a land of freedom, their heart cry is like that of Patrick Henry of revolutionary days, "Give me liberty or give me death!" Americans first and soldiers second, they are demonstrating to the Iraqi people what American freedom means.

The April 4, 2003, edition of the *Amarillo Globe News* carried an Associated Press story that tells of Corporal Nicholas Beitia, 22, of Elko, Nevada. "At first I hated these people," acknowledged Beitia, but his attitude changed in his first house-to-house search. First the civilians were terrified, apparently assuming that he intended to murder the men, rape the women, and plunder the home. "Then I got down on my knee and gave their little girl a piece of chewing gum," he related. "The father was ecstatic. It was like I was saying I was not better than them. When I got down on my knee, they almost started to cry. They brought us tea. There was a daughter in the house who could speak some English, and they gave us some fresh pita bread."

On the same day, 150 hard-line Iraqi fighters stationed themselves inside the Mosque of Ali in Najaf, Iraq. When U.S. troops approached, local citizens were outraged that they might enter the Shiite Muslim shrine. Under the wise leadership of their commander, the troops went to their knees, placed their guns on the ground, thus diffusing the tension. More than national leaders could ever do, our young warriors demonstrate to the world what it means to be an American and to live in the land of freedom.

The resolution of the Iraqi conflict will not end tensions in the Middle East. The anger, hatred, frustrations, and resentments that precipitated recent terrorist attacks throughout the world, including the destruction of the Twin Towers in New York City, pervades the Arab world. Long standing animosity between Muslims and Jews has reached the boiling point. America, which the Arabs identify with Israel, has become the focal point of Arab animosity. Spiritual struggles between Judaism, Christianity, and Islam undermine any apparent possibility of reconciliation. Predating the birth of Christ, these struggles have intensified because of Jewish presence in the Holy Land, which the Muslims claim as their own, and because of increased Christian and American influence. But this is now a third millennium issue that will be addressed in my second book.

The wars that America has fought have clearly demonstrated the hand of God upon this nation. If this were not so, America would never have survived the War of Independence and the War of 1812. It would likely have split into two nations in the Civil War, and it would never have been victorious in World War II when, in one battle after another, the outcome of the war appeared to be in the balance.

The man lifted his eyes to his heavenly Father and said, "I see the paradox of this nation. Daily, Mexicans wade the Rio Grande River and slip across the border to come to America. There are more applications for immigration to this country than can be handled. And yet America has such a dark history in its treatment of blacks and Native American Indians. I see how Marshall enforced the purpose of the Supreme Court. And yet the same court has systematically led the nation away from its divine calling. I see the recurring struggle in one war after another. And yet you have protected this nation from destruction from forces within and without."

And the Father replied, "This nation will struggle to define itself. That struggle is centered in its purpose and its call as one nation set apart to Me. That struggle involves every dimension of the American way of life and the perception of its citizens. It is a struggle for a nation and its people to determine why it was established and what it is called to be. It is the call to destiny. In every area in which this nation turns away from my call—my plan—my purpose—the struggle will be manifest over and over again. The same problem will recur until or unless it comes in accord with my call for this nation. Do not forget that this nation is special to Me; it was established by my covenant with your forefathers; it was preserved as a land of promise. But when much is given, much is expected. This nation has a destiny to fulfill my plan for it and for the whole world. Continue to seek a revelation of my destiny for this nation as I call it forth as a Nation under God."

Chapter 11

MANIFEST DESTINY

as proclaimed by American lawyer/writer, John L. O'Sullivan

Before the Mexican War: *"The far-reaching, the boundless future will be the era of American greatness. In its magnificent domain of space and time, the nation of many nations is destined to manifest to mankind the excellence of divine principles; to establish on earth the noblest temple ever dedicated to the worship of the Most High . . ."*

After the annexation of Texas: *". . . the inevitable fulfillment of the general law which is rolling our population westward—the connection of which with that ratio of growth in population . . . is too evident to leave us in doubt of the manifest design of Providence in regard to the occupation of this continent."*

During the debate over the future of the Oregon territory: *"And yet after all, unanswerable as is the demonstration of our legal title to Oregon . . . that claim is by the right of our manifest destiny to overspread and to possess the whole continent which Providence has given us for the development of the great experiment of liberty and federated self-government entrusted to us."* [149]

MANIFEST DESTINY

In 1818 Spain claimed Florida as a territory. The Spanish maintained two token garrisons at San Marcos in east Florida and San Michel in west Florida; but the real nations in control of Florida were the Seminole and Creek Indian tribes. It was a practice of these two tribes to sneak out of Florida, steal cattle and goods, and kill and scalp anyone who stood in their way.[150]

The United States government did not permit any U.S. military force to enter the Spanish Florida territory for fear of Spanish reprisal. In 1818 Andrew Jackson, with questionable authority from President Monroe, entered Florida, routed the Indians, and stormed Fort San Michel. Without a single shot fired at the fort, the Spanish governor of Florida surrendered, thus creating a crisis with Spain.[151] In order to resolve this conflict, President Monroe called on John Quincy Adams to bargain with the Spaniards, who first insisted that the Americans punish Jackson. Because of Adams's uncompromising negotiation, the Spaniards finally agreed to accept $5 million in damages and yield to the United States all claims to Florida. Additionally, in return for the Texas territory and recognition of Spanish rights to California, Spain relinquished all of its claims to the rest of what would become the United States of America.[152] Later, Mexico ousted Spain from Mexico and claimed the California territory.

In 1803 Jefferson's administration negotiated the Louisiana Purchase with France, which included the Mississippi River Valley and New Orleans, for $15 million. By this one purchase, France was removed as a primary colonial force in America.[153] Now this nation was ready to proclaim its *manifest destiny,*" as would later be proclaimed by John L. O'Sullivan, to "possess the whole continent which Providence has given us."[154]

And west they went. In early days the settlers moved west from Virginia and the Carolinas into Tennessee and Kentucky. There they became expert marksmen by fighting the Indians and the animals in the wild natural surroundings, which may have saved the nation in the Battle of New Orleans at the end of the War of 1812. Farmers left their barren rocky farmland in the Northeast and traveled west to the fertile farmland of the Ohio Valley. By the late 1790s and early 1800s, there was a steady stream of Americans heading west for new life and prosperity. Many settled east of the Mississippi River, and then west of that great river. Every place of settlement was a challenge because of the Native American Indians and the cruel natural forces. But on they came, more and more, a steady rumble of wagons and horses, looking for a new home.

Travelers to the West brought back reports of the fertile valleys of Oregon, which was like the new Eden that would produce all crops. And so these Americans began their trek across the Continental Divide to the West, heading for Oregon, even though, according to treaty, the British and the Americans jointly owned it. A few headed west to California, despite the fact that it was owned by Mexico; America was ready to stretch from the Atlantic to the Pacific.

The trip across the Continental Divide was the most difficult journey for these American adventurers. It was impossible to cross the Rockies during the winter. Those traveling through the Rockies had to plan their trip carefully in order to complete their passage before the snow began to fall. Along each of the mountain passes were the graves of those who were not strong enough, or too late in their passage, or killed by the Indians.

The greatest struggle for westward expansion was with the Indians, which meant expulsion of tribes. Many Native American Indians fought back, but some did not. Many trusted the Americans when treaties were offered because they believed that what a man said was true. They did not fight back until they saw that these new Americans could not be trusted to keep their promises. Therefore, there was a constant confrontation between the Indians who sought to preserve their land and the new Americans who sought to take it.[155]

The dispossession of the indigenous people of this nation is a blight on the history of the United States of America. As the Americans traveled west, they were willing to do anything that was necessary to take the land that was before them. The same spirit of adventure that brought them and their forefathers to America led them to kill or dispossess the Native American Indians who stood in their way. They often viewed these Indians as an obstacle to civilization and the development of the land. The attitude of many settlers was expressed by L. Frank Baum, author of *The Wizard of Oz,* when he wrote in 1890:

> With his fall the nobility of the Redskin is extinguished, and what few are left are a pack of whining curs who lick the hand that smites them. The whites, by law of conquest and by justice of civilization, are master of the American continent, and the best safety of the frontier settlements will be secured by the total annihilation of the few remaining Indians.[156]

Many historians estimate the Indian population before Columbus at ten to twelve million; by 1900 only 237,000 Native American Indians were left in the United States. In the early 1800s California's Indian population was estimated at 260,000; by the year 1900 that population was reduced to 20,000. As the native population was driven from the land, 23 percent were placed on reservations and the balance moved to urban areas. Except for their almost intolerable life on reservations, these first Americans were effectively driven from all of the land.[157] Today, more than 150 years later, many of the once proud Indian nations have been reduced to life on reservations, which has produced a high incidence of hopelessness, despair, and alcoholism.

The prizes of the expansion to the west were Texas and California. In the early 1800s Texas belonged to Mexico. In 1812 a group of Mexicans and Americans marched from Louisiana, took San Antonio, and set up the State of Texas. They were wiped out by a Spanish force. A second group of exiles set up a Texas Republic in 1818, and a third republic was proclaimed in 1819. In the meantime, the Spanish forces were dispossessed by a Mexican government, and Texas became a Mexican territory.[158]

When the Mexican government could not control the west Texas territory and the Comanche and other Indian tribes, they invited Stephen Austin to bring Americans into Texas to settle the land. The tolerant Mexican government permitted the American-Texas frontiersmen to develop unhindered and to establish a *de facto* self-government.

Eventually, the Mexican government's indulgent attitude changed, and in 1830 all Anglo immigration to Texas was stopped. The Mexican authorities also made it clear that they intended to stop self-government in Texas.

The Texans were always fiercely independent, with an intense hatred of the Mexicans. The Comanches shared that hatred and attacked the Mexicans, but, out of respect for the bravery and expert marksmanship of these settlers, spared the Anglo-Texans.

In 1830, the Mexican government, under the new leadership of Santa Anna, closed Texas to all further Anglo immigration. Santa

Anna also made it clear that he intended to end Texan self-government. When the Texans protested, the centralist government threatened to disarm them by force. The Texans then organized a militia for self-defense, and a minor clash followed, with Texans taking a Mexican fort. When the Texans refused to surrender, the men involved in the uprising, including Stephen Austin, were arrested and held in a Mexico City jail, without a trial, for one and one-half years. When he was released in 1835, the Texans were ready to fight. Mexico planned a military advance into Texas, and the Texans called on other Americans to come to their defense.[159]

Santa Anna advanced on the small Texas army, and the point of attack was a mission in San Antonio called the Alamo. A song that was popular in the mid-twentieth century described the bravery of the Texans at the Alamo as follows:

A hundred and eighty were challenged by Travis to die.
A line that he drew with his sword when the battle was nigh.
'The man who would fight to the death cross over
but he who that would live better fly.'
And over the line stepped a hundred and seventy-nine.[160]

The story of the Alamo has been told so many times that it and the men who died there have been firmly established in the legends and folklore of this nation. When the battle was over, all of the Texans in the Alamo, who apparently totaled 187, were dead. But they were surrounded by the bodies of over 1,000 Mexican soldiers, and there were many more dead Mexican soldiers outside the Alamo. The total number of Mexicans that the Texans killed exceeded 1,600, and there were an additional 500 wounded Mexican soldiers left behind.[161] By legend, the number of Texans who died in the Alamo was more than those defending the Alamo, because other Americans slipped in to join in the fight after the Alamo's fate was determined. To add to the folklore, the dead defenders of the Alamo included Jim Bowie, Davy Crockett, and others who were men of legend before they came to Texas.

Santa Anna and the Mexican Army then moved to Goliad, where the rest of the Texas Army, consisting of 500 men, was stationed. When the Mexicans closed in on Colonel Fannin and his men at Goliad, and began to fire from all sides, Fannin surrendered unconditionally. Santa Anna marched the able-bodied men out of town and shot them. Then he dragged wounded prisoners into the streets and shot them all. The Texas battle cries then became "Remember the Alamo" and "Remember Goliad."

Eventually, Sam Houston built an army, which lured Santa Anna deeper into Texas away from his supply lines. Houston attacked Santa Anna's forces during their afternoon siesta and routed the Mexican Army. The Mexican losses totaled 630 dead and 600 captured, compared to two Texans killed and twenty-four wounded. Santa Anna ordered his Mexican troops out of Texas across the Rio Grande. Through this one victory, the Republic of Texas was created.[162] The fighting was over in seven weeks. An election was held, and Sam Houston became Texas's first president.[163]

When Santa Anna returned to Mexico, humiliated by Sam Houston's out-manned army, he went into exile. In 1838 he reemerged to lead the Mexican Army to war against the Texans.[164]

In 1842 Santa Anna incited a full-scale border war with Texas in order to rally the Mexican people behind him. When reports reached America of Santa Anna's atrocities, President Polk chose this time for America to participate in the Texans' fight with Mexico.

President Polk had received reports from the settlers in California describing that land as a paradise, a land of awesome beauty where everything grew. In Washington D.C., in the press, and in the halls of Congress, there were those who were talking of expansion to the Pacific as this nation's "manifest destiny." President Polk recognized that the destiny of this nation was to spread from sea to sea and was willing to engage Mexico to accomplish that end. Therefore, when Santa Anna started a border war with Texas, he played into Polk's hands.[165]

Polk sent General Zachary Taylor and his Louisiana detachment to the Rio Grande for the express purpose of ensuring the safety of American citizens, but Taylor was also instructed to engage the Mexican forces if necessary.

When Taylor's forces reached the Rio Grande, they faced a much larger Mexican army than expected, with more reinforcements coming. When all of the Mexican forces arrived, the Americans were outnumbered two to one, and in a difficult strategic position. When Taylor sent a request for support from the Texans, the first to appear were seventy-seven Texas Rangers led by their captain, Sam Walker. The Rangers were organized in 1835 when the Republic of Texas was fighting for her life. Taylor's army, consisting of West Point trainees who were disciplined but untested, observed the Texas Rangers and decided that they were without discipline and would be a detriment to any detachment to which they were assigned.

Each of the Texas Rangers had two curved-handled revolvers as side arms, which Captain Sam Walker had designed. Walker had ordered a thousand of the legendary Walker Colt revolvers from his friend, Samuel Colt. The revolvers were specially designed for quick use and easy reloading at full gallop.

As Taylor and his soldiers watched the Rangers care for their horses and prepare for battle, they concluded that their first impressions were wrong, and that these men were no ordinary soldiers.

The importance of Walker and his Texas Rangers was soon apparent. When Taylor was trying to determine the strength, location, and movement of the Mexican Army, Sam Walker took four of his companions for reconnaissance through the enemy line to gain this information. The reconnaissance efforts of the Texas Rangers and the masterful leadership of General Taylor produced an American victory against more than two-to-one odds. When the first battle was over, the Mexican Army decamped in the night to a new fortified position. Taylor's army waited on the Rangers' reconnaissance patrols to report the Mexican Army movement, and then followed to engage them at their new location. When the second battle ended, the Mexican Army was routed and fled for their lives. The Mexicans lost 2,000 men over the two-day battle, compared to 170 American losses.[166]

The battles between Taylor's troops and the Mexican Army set the pattern for the Mexican War. Since the Americans were fighting on Mexican soil, the Mexican Army always had a large numerical and strategic advantage. The Mexican soldiers were well-trained, courageous soldiers, but time and time again, because of their skillful reconnaissance, the Americans were able to position forces for a surprise attack that routed and demoralized the Mexican Army. In every battle, the Mexican losses were many times those of the Americans.

Two young men who served under Taylor's command became renowned men of battle; they were Sam Grant and Robert E. Lee. Sam Grant, who was later known by his name Ulysses S. Grant, was a celebrated horseman. On one occasion, he rode through the streets of Monterrey, hanging on the side of his horse for protection from enemy fire, to inform Taylor of the condition of the army and its need for ammunition and support.[167]

Robert E. Lee was a young captain whose specialty was reconnaissance. Several times Lee found passageways to strategic points behind the enemy lines that permitted the Americans to outflank or outmaneuver the Mexicans by a surprise attack from the rear. On one occasion, Lee was at a spring when a group of Mexican soldiers appeared. Lee hid under a fallen tree while some of the Mexican soldiers sat on it. Throughout the day and into the night, Lee lay motionless, with ants and spiders crawling on him. Finally, after nightfall he was able to escape.[168]

Grant and Lee would meet in the major battles of the Civil War, with Lee leading the Confederates and Grant as commanding general of the Northern Army. Grant would later serve as an American president after the Civil War.

Perhaps the most heroic victories were carried out by the First Missouri Mounted Volunteers, led by Colonel William Doniphan. The Missourians traveled from Ft. Leavenworth across the hot, barren New Mexico land and through rough and sandy terrain, where there were few water holes, until they finally arrived at Santa Fe, which they took without firing a shot. Their boots were not made for infantry duty, but they continued on and could be tracked by their bloody footprints left in the sand.

From Santa Fe, they traveled south across the dry wasteland known as the Jornada del Muerto, the Journey of Death, which was a ninety-mile trek across a desert without any water. Weakened by the trip, but without any loss of lives, part of Doniphan's troops, totaling 500 men, reached El Paso, where they faced the Mexican Army of 1,300 men. The Missourians defeated the Mexican Army without loss of life, but now Doniphan received word that the Mexican forces were rallying at Chihuahua. He led the Missourians across another desert that was worse than anything they had faced, with sand in drifts like snow. Their canteens were dry, the wagons sank in the sand, the mules were too weak to pull the wagons, and the men had to work side by side with the animals to move the wagons. Finally, when the troops were only ten miles away from water, the army came to a stop. They could go no farther and prepared to die, as buzzards flew overhead. Suddenly above the distant mountains appeared one cloud and another, and then came a torrential rain. Soon there were gullies and puddles everywhere. Each man drank to his fill and watered and cared for the animals. Refreshed, they rode on to engage the Mexican Army at Chihuahua.

The Mexican Army at Chihuahua totaled more than 4,000, while Doniphan arrived with just over 900 soldiers and 150 teamsters. The Mexicans dug in and were ready for battle. However, Doniphan was an innovator. He suddenly moved his entire army laterally and up onto a plateau beside the Mexican position. Now the enemy would have to leave their fortification and come out and fight. Confused by this tactic, the Mexican cavalry charged the American lines. Even though Doniphan had traveled across the desert wasteland, he arrived with enough artillery to seize the moment. With six field guns loaded with grapeshot, the Americans began rapid firing at an astonishing twelve seconds per round. Before the Mexican charge reached the American lines, it was broken. The Missourians then mounted their own charge and routed the Mexican Army. The casualties sustained by the Missourians were one dead and eleven wounded.

The Missourians returned home as conquering national heroes. They had traveled 6,000 miles and conquered an area larger than the United States.

Finally, victory over Santa Anna and the Mexican Army was secured in Mexico City in September 1847. In February 1848 the Treaty of Guadalupe Hidalgo was signed, which ceded to the United States the Republic of Texas, California, and New Mexico. The New Mexico and California territories included Arizona, Nevada, New

Mexico, California, Utah, and parts of Colorado and Wyoming. In exchange, the Mexican government received $15 million plus $3.25 million in cancellation of outstanding claims of American citizens against Mexico.[169]

President Polk also received reports of the rich farm land of Oregon. With the cry of "manifest destiny" ringing throughout the nation, the House of Representatives voted 163 to 54 to end the joint occupancy treaty with Britain and to claim Oregon as a territory. Since Britain was embroiled in other wars, and because of its prior battles with America, it sought compromise. A new line was drawn on the 49th parallel between American and British territories that gave Oregon to the United States.[170]

The man pondered these events. The Mexican Army was a formidable army of brave soldiers. Yet in every battle the outnumbered Americans were victorious, with minimal loss of life. God's divine intervention was seen, as well as the brilliance of the American military leaders. The man raised his eyes to heaven and said, "Father, I see that you were faithful in your covenant to the land. And I look with pride at what our forefathers have done to establish this nation as one nation under God."

And the Father spoke, "You take pride in the indomitable American spirit, but look closer. The nature of a nation is determined by the conduct of those who control it. In this land of choice, the nature of the nation will be set by the manner in which its people exercise freedom.

"And what is the spirit of a nation that takes what it wants because it has the power to do so? And what is the nature of a nation that dispossesses those who were there first without even a thought? And what is the spirit of a nation that makes heroes of the strong and mighty and forgets the One who established it?

"The choices made by those in this land of promise will determine the spirit of this land, for the essence of freedom is the choice made and the consequence of that choice."

Chapter 12

Can I see anothers woe,
And not be in sorrow too.
Can I see anothers grief,
And not seek for kind relief.

Can I see a falling tear,
And not feel my sorrows share.
Can a father see his child,
Weep, nor be with sorrow fill'd.

Can a mother sit and hear,
An infant groan an infant fear—
No no never can it be.
Never never can it be.

And can he who smiles on all
Hear the wren with sorrows small,
Hear the small birds grief & care
Hear the woes that infants bear—

And not sit beside the nest
Pouring pity in their breast,
And not sit the cradle near
Weeping tear on infants tear.

And not sit both night & day,
Wiping all our tears away . . .

—*Songs of Innocence and of Experience* by William Blake

THE SUFFERING SERVANTS

How can one describe the effect of slavery in this new land of promise? How can one take another as his property and control his will, his action, and his life? How can a people buy and sell another nation of people as you would sell a swine or a horse or an ox? What is the effect of slavery on the one who is enslaved? What is the consequence of slavery to those who enslave?

The seafaring Portuguese first began modern-day slave trade in the fifteenth century on the North African coast. The Portuguese established slave trade in their Southern territory of Brazil, and it spread over South America.[171]

In 1619 the first North American slaves were purchased by Virginians from a Dutch man-of-war. The twenty "negars" that were purchased were told they would be freed after five years of indentured servitude. That same year, the Virginia colony transported ninety young women to the colony for sale to any bachelor who would pay the cost of transportation, set at 125 pounds of tobacco. Also at this time, Virginia established a representative form of government; however, only free, white, property-owning men could vote.

The transportation of large numbers of black slaves to America did not begin in North America until the eighteenth century.[172] The popularity of tobacco in Europe led the Virginia farmers to use all cleared ground to plant it; but tobacco leached the nutrients out of the land, and it became necessary to clear more. This, in turn, increased the demand for labor. A system of indenture developed whereby laborers agreed to work for four to five years in exchange for their passage to America. Since those laborers were freed from their servitude too soon to satisfy the Virginia farmers, the idea of slaves for life developed. In 1661 Virginia officially recognized the institution of slavery. Less than one century later there were 120,000 blacks in Virginia and 173,000 whites. By 1790, when the first national census was taken, the five states of Maryland, Virginia, the Carolinas, and Georgia had a slave population of 1,100,000. "Triangular trade" became prominent. The slave coast of Africa was controlled by black tribes who raided other tribes and sold them to the Yankee slave traders in exchange for rum. The white slave traders took their black slave merchandise to the West Indies, where they sold many of the slaves for molasses, which was used to make more rum. The Yankee slave traders then sold the rest of their slaves on the American coast and took the molasses to New England. There they exchanged molasses for rum and returned to Africa for more slaves.

Slave ships were constructed with compartments no larger than a coffin where the slaves were required to lie shackled for the entire voyage. More than 50 percent died at sea and were thrown overboard. Since there was so much profit, the high death rate did not discourage the slave traders, who tried to cram more slaves on board for the next voyage. After Eli Whitney invented the cotton gin, the demand for slaves increased. By the time of the Missouri debates, the number of slaves in the South increased to 1,500,000, which was one slave for every two Southern whites.[173]

The treatment of slaves as property in this land of freedom, without the respect normally accorded even to beasts of burden, is a part of our history that Americans would like to forget. But history reminds us of the cruel overseer with his black whip swinging through the air to strike the naked back of an unruly slave; the family tearfully clinging to each other for the last time when they were sold to different owners at the slave auctions; the Southern lady of the house politely ignoring the coincidence of a red-headed child of a slave girl when her husband was the only redhead in the county; the "poor white trash" who purchased a slave that he could curse and abuse in order to prove that he was important; and the constant physical and verbal abuse of these blacks who were considered less than beasts of burden.

But could it be that the slave owners became the slaves trapped in their own oppressive system? Slavery resulted in the gradual economic and societal regression back to the equivalent of the feudal states of medieval England. The incentive of the Southerners was destroyed because a true Southern gentlemen did not work with his hands. As one visitor observed:

> The whites stand with their hands in their pockets, and the blacks are helping them do nothing. Fences are down, doors ajar, filth in the streets, foul odors in the air, confusion and neglect are everywhere. Go into a [planter's] house late at night and they are all lounging about, too lazy to go to bed. Go in the morning, they are all yawning in bed, too lazy to get up. No one has his prescribed duties—the master scolds and drives, the slave dawdles and shirks.[174]

The slaves actually set the pace for the jobs in the battle of will between the owners and the slaves.[175] Not only were slave owners prisoners of their own system but so was all of the South. The system did away with a middle class leaving only the rich, who would not labor, the very poor, and the slaves who had to labor for both.[176] Senator W. C. Preston of South Carolina reported his journey north:

> No Southern man can journey, as I have lately done, through the Northern States and witness the prosperity, the industry, the public spirit which they exhibit . . . without feelings of deep sadness and shame, as he remembers his own neglected and desolate home. . . . [In the North] no

dwelling is to be seen abandoned, no farm uncultivated . . .
The whole land is covered with fertile fields, with manu-
factories, and canals, and railroads, and edifices, and towns,
and cities. Along the route of the great New York canal . . .
a canal, a railroad, and a turnpike are to be seen in the width
of perhaps a hundred yards, each of them crowded with
travel, or overflowing with commerce . . . Passing along [the
canal], you see no space of three miles without a town or
village, and you are never out of the sound of a church
bell . . . How different the condition of these things in the
South! Here, the face of the country wears the aspect of
premature old age and decay. No improvement is seen going
on—nothing is done for prosperity—no man thinks of
anything beyond the present moment. Our lands are yearly
tasked to their utmost capacity of production, and when
exhausted, are abandoned for the youthful West.[177]

The fact that one man was master over another extended not
only to the slave quarters but also to other Southern businesses that
employed poor whites. The son of a Southern planter sadly recalled:

An unconquerable pride grew up in the hearts of this class—
the pride of unchallenged domination, of irresponsible
control of others, of unquestioned power, of uncriticized
conduct. Each man became a lord within his own domain.
He was the source of law among his slaves, and his self-interest
and good or ill will was the rule of his actions; the laws of the
State did not readily reach him, and public opinion of his
own class naturally coincided with his views. There thus
resulted an absolute indifference to the opinions of others.[178]

When the price of cotton dropped, the Southern planters became slaves of their own system. The continued decline in the world-wide price of cotton so depressed the market that even the richest planters mortgaged their crops, leaving their slaves as their only wealth.[179]

It seemed that the life of the slave owner subtly destroyed every fabric of that enterprising nature that established this nation. While traveling in the South, John Bernard, manager of Federal Street Theatre in Philadelphia, described the typical slave owner:

> During the summer he used to rise about nine, when he exerted himself to walk as far as his stables to look at the stud which he kept for the races. At ten, he breakfasted on coffee, eggs, and hoe-cake, concluding it with the commencement of his diurnal potions—a stiff glass of mint-sling [julep]—a disorder peculiar to the South. He then sought the coolest room and stretched himself on a pallet in his shirt and trousers, with a negress at his head and another at his feet to keep off the flies and promote reflection. Between twelve and one, he would sip half a pint of some mystery termed bumbo, apple-toddy, or pumpkin flip. He then mounted a pony and with an umbrella over his head, rode gently around his estate to converse with his overseers. At three, he dined and drank everything—brandy, claret, cider, Madeira, punch, and sangaree, then resumed his pallet with his negresses, and meditated until teatime.[180]

The South and the slave owners were driven by fear—a soul-shaking fear of the day of judgment because of the slave system; a fear of uprising by the slaves; a fear of keeping the slaves; a fear of setting them free. Fear was the key factor in Southern life during all of the years of slavery.[181]

In order to preserve a system that was about to destroy them, the Southerners went to great lengths to defend it. Many planters believed that God put blacks on the earth to serve whites. They called slaves the descendants of Cain cursed with dark skin.[182] It seemed the South was willing to ignore slavery as if it were no issue. With the Church and anti-slavery groups of the North decrying the inhumanity of slavery, the South was forced to reconsider. Southern newspaper editors began to revive the slavery question by presenting the evils of slavery. Soon the attitude of the South hardened into the cruelest of all positions, as expressed by William and Mary College Professor William Dew—the slaves had no redeeming social value and were placed on earth by God to serve white men. Dew presented his thesis that slavery was "perhaps the principal means for impelling forward the civilization of mankind." He concluded that slaves were lazy shifters, thievish, and incapable of caring for themselves, and that slave holders had the solemn responsibility to look after them.[183] The South picked up these arguments, which found their way into the battle cries leading up to the Civil War—"how can we turn these slaves loose on society?"

The conclusion that slaves were inferior has had devastating consequences in this nation and particularly in the South. After slavery ended, blacks were denied access to whites' schools; they were not allowed to enter the whites' restaurants; they could not use whites-only toilets, and if there were no toilets for blacks they had to seek other choices; they were required to sit at the back of the bus; they could not attend colleges, except the inferior black schools. They were verbally abused because of their golden, black, and brown skin. Surprisingly, this discrimination continued for a century after the Civil War, and there is still evidence of such discrimination throughout America today.

However, there was a destiny for African Americans, which was a critical part of the destiny of America. Even though most of their ancestors had never heard of Christianity, they quickly became converts; in the midst of their suffering they were sustained by their faith in the Lord Jesus Christ. The more they were persecuted, the greater their faith. In the early-morning hours and late at night, while their weary bodies moved slowly to and from the fields, they sang songs of faith. Whenever possible, they assembled to sing and worship and to share their love of the Lord Jesus Christ.

Most slave owners denied their slaves the right to practice their faith, and so the black church went underground. They met in secret places in the woods, singing hymns at a whisper. They were willing to risk discovery and punishment in order to share their Christian faith with their brothers. The slaves developed codes to signal to each other their meeting places. The well-known spiritual hymn "Steal Away to Jesus" was often a signal for a clandestine meeting.[184]

The slaves prayed for the sick and the hurting, but they also prayed for freedom. As they prayed, they beseeched the Lord to deliver them from slavery, but they also looked to their heavenly deliverance. "Soon, very soon, they were going to see the King"; all pain and sorrow would end when they got to the other side. Their faith and their songs sustained them in the long dreary days of slavery.

Isaiah prophesied about the Son of God, the Crucified One, as follows:

He grew up before him like a tender shoot, and like a root out of dry ground. He had no beauty or majesty to attract us to him, nothing in his appearance that we should desire him. He was despised and rejected by men, a man of sorrows, and familiar with suffering. Like one from whom men hide their faces he was despised, and we esteemed him not. Surely he took up our infirmities and carried our sorrows, yet we considered him stricken by God, smitten by him, and afflicted.

—Isaiah 53:2–4 NIV

In America in the days of slavery, the blacks were the suffering servants, so like the Lord Jesus Christ whom they served. In the days after they were liberated from slavery, the faith of these suffering servants was demonstrated in their determination to make a place for their families in America. And so mothers, determined that their children should have better opportunities, labored long hours at low pay under demeaning circumstances without a word of protest. Black fathers labored at a fraction of the pay afforded whites to provide a small home and the simplest provisions for their families. For years they educated their children in separate schools with inferior facilities and educational tools, while white students attended large, well-equipped schools, paid for by taxpayers. Repeatedly, they and their children were called names and cursed and forced to take demeaning positions for only one reason—they were black.

With a quiet determination, these blacks began to demand equality. With faces set like flint, black mothers walked their children to white schools demanding admission in the midst of curses, abuse, and physical violence. Young students marched to white colleges demanding the right to attend. No longer were they willing to accept "separate but equal" schools and other facilities, which were often grossly unequal. Finally blacks began to emerge from the frustration at the slow pace of their acquisition of civil rights. In Montgomery, Alabama, on December 1, 1955, Rosa Parks, a black woman, refused to give up her bus seat to a white rider, thereby defying the Southern custom that required blacks to yield their seats at the front of the bus to whites. When she was jailed, a black boycott led by Martin Luther King Jr.

began and lasted a year. The Montgomery boycott was followed by the first anti-segregation sit-in on February 1, 1960, in Greensboro, North Carolina. Demonstrations continued, culminating in a mass demonstration in black communities throughout the nation on August 28, 1963, and a march of 250,000 protestors led by King to the steps of the Lincoln Memorial in Washington, D.C., where King delivered a memorable oration: "I have a dream that my four little children will one day live in a nation where they will be judged not by the color of their skin, but by . . . their character."[185]

One hundred fifty years after they were liberated under the leadership of President Abraham Lincoln, African Americans still fight to be treated as equals. Although they have made some gains, they are far from equal treatment in every area of life and labor. For over two centuries they have suffered—first as slaves and then as freed citizens treated as slaves.

The man considered the plight of these suffering servants and lifted his eyes to the Father and said, "Now I understand the indomitable American spirit. It is not the spirit of the strong and mighty. It is the unwavering spirit of the meek and the lowly that has made this nation great."

And the Father replied, "My eyes are fixed on those suffering servants who turned to my Son in their times of trial. And I have heard their cry. Look closely, my son. See what has happened in the place of their suffering. There, the faith of this nation has been sustained. And why do you think that is true? Is my hand on the strong and the mighty, or do they have their own reward? I make a covenant with those who call upon the name of my Son in the days of their suffering. My covenant is with the suffering ones and the land they call home. It is not the proud and arrogant for whom I have blessed and preserved the nation. My eyes are fixed on the meek and the lowly. For them I have blessed this nation.

Chapter 13

And so the Word had breath, and wrought
With human hands the creed of creeds
In loveliness of perfect deeds,
More strong than all poetic thought.

Ring in the valiant man and free,
The larger heart, the kindlier hand;
Ring out the darkness of the land,
Ring in the Christ that is to be.

—from *In Memoriam A. H. H.*, by Alfred, Lord Tennyson,
an English poet, in 1849 and 1850

THE EVENT OF THE CENTURY

I n the late 1850s, America experienced unparalleled financial success. The nation was moving west, with the participation of the railroad and the telegraph. The vast resources of the Great Plains, minerals unearthed in the mountains, and gold discovered on the West Coast pushed the United States to the forefront of the industrial revolution. President Buchanan, in his inaugural address, spoke of the financial success of the nation as follows: "No nation has ever before been embarrassed from too large a surplus in its treasury."[186]

But there were signs of concern. For more than a decade, religious life in the United States of America was declining. In the years between 1845 and 1857, increase of membership in the Christian denominations scarcely kept pace with the death losses; the issue of slavery was becoming predominant in the nation; scandals were occurring in the nation to such extent that President Buchanan, in his inaugural address, referred to "a corruption which thrived when love of money had usurped the proper place of public virtue."[187] The nation was moving west as fortune-seekers went to Texas, California, and other states; however, poverty flourished, and workers were willing to work for less than a dollar a day. The poverty of the South was institutionalized in its slavery, while Northern citizens were making money very easily in boom times.[188]

Heman Humphrey, president of Amherst College, commented on the state of the church:

Many churches here and there were refreshed and many souls brought in. To an alarming extent the young were growing up without hope and without God in the world. There was increasing coldness and worldly conformity in the churches . . . It was very dark and it seemed to be growing darker. A money mania pervaded not only all our commercial cities, but the whole country, more or less.[189]

In the midst of prosperity, a strange economic crisis developed. In the summer of 1857 America was caught up in speculative investments brought about by the westward expansion of the nation. Bogus land developments were reaping fortunes, speculating on the next city that would emerge in the West. On the plains of Kansas and other states, mystical cities were laid out and lots sold to Easterners at exorbitant prices. So vast and numerous were these blueprint cities, they covered as much territory as all of the real cities in the North and the middle states combined. Fortunes were made overnight; and even conservative financiers began to lose perspective. Even though there were clear signs that the boom was slowing, banks and others continued to engage in speculation.[190]

Finally, in August of 1857, the collapse of the economy began in the failure of a large and trusted Ohio bank. Suddenly people everywhere began to wonder if their own banks were safe and decided to withdraw their money, only to find that the banks did not have sufficient funds. The ensuing nationwide panic precipitated such a run on the banks that the entire system collapsed. The stock market crashed, factories closed, and unemployment soared. In New York City 30,000 men were out of work, and angry mobs roamed the streets.[191] Eighteen of the leading banks of New York were compelled to halt financial operations. On October 14, 1857, the extensive banking system of the United States of America collapsed, bringing ruin to the citizens of New York, Philadelphia, Boston, and the industrial centers of the nation.[192] Men of vast wealth awoke to find that their wealth was gone; many Wall Street financiers became instant paupers. Unable to face the prospect of financial destruction, some took their own lives. Since there was nothing intrinsically wrong with the economy, the financial collapse did not last. In less than six months, the economy had regained its strength, and the banks reopened by December, but the crisis shook the nation.[193]

And then came a revival that J. Edwin Orr referred to as "The Event of the Century." Although it seemed to erupt abruptly, the seed of revival had been planted years before. By the 1840s a noticeable decline in the spiritual condition of the nation had occurred. *The New York Observer* ran articles in 1844 bemoaning the lack of revival, declaring: "Dear Christian bretheren, we must have revivals . . . or we are undone."[194] Many of the faithful continued to pray for revival and undergirded their petitions with personal repentance.

An appeal for revival was made in the Methodist church and other denominations. In 1857, the *Baptist Watchman* of Boston devoted its publication to the prayer movement that was then occurring in New England. Under the heading "Time of Refreshing," the *New York Observer* noticed religious sentiment reemerging throughout the nation. Intercession increased among various denominations preceding a week of revival in Boston. Leaders of the Presbyterians, Baptists, and other Protestant denominations joined together in a movement of prayer that spread throughout New York, Boston, Philadelphia, Ohio, and other places.[195] Revival dramatically occurred among the slaves in the South, who were increasingly involved in the movement of intercession for revival. A "remarkable revival" occurred in the Anson Street Presbyterian Church in Charleston, South Carolina, where forty-eight blacks and approximately one dozen white members gathered for prayer. In response to a call for a spiritual awakening, attendance increased at the Anson Street Church until the sanctuary was filled. Pastor John L. Girardeau was urged to begin preaching, but he declined, "waiting for the outpouring of the Spirit." One evening, while leading the petitioners in prayer, he received a sensation, as if a surge of electric power had struck his body:

> For a little while, he stood speechless under the strange physical feeling. Then he said: "The Holy Spirit has come. We will begin preaching tomorrow evening." He closed the service with a hymn and dismissed the congregation, and came down from the pulpit; but no one left the house. The whole congregation had quietly resumed its seats. Instantly he realized the situation. The Holy Spirit had not only come to him, He had also taken possession of the hearts of the people.[196]

Girardeau preached nightly to crowds numbering 1,500 to 2,000 for eight full weeks; he called this "the greatest event in my ministry." In Maryland, Virginia, and the Carolinas, revival spread among the blacks.[197]

Throughout 1857 revival fires spread throughout the nation. Boston's *Watchman* and *Reflector* reported revivals in churches in Massachusetts, Rhode Island, Brooklyn, and in New York City. The president of Amherst College reported revivals on his campus, and half of the student body of Yale was converted.[198] The clergy of Boston invited the aging Charles Finney to conduct a six-week campaign at Park Street Church. God honored Finney's obedience by pouring out His Spirit, and the Park Street Church became a spiritual powerhouse lighting up most of Boston.[199]

During the summer, unusual revivals occurred in Minnesota; Dutchess County, New York; Virginia; Boston; Missouri; South Carolina; and many other places. A Presbyterian church in Tennessee experienced "the most interesting and effective meeting ever known in the history of our denomination in this part of the world." Seven camp meetings held near Manor Hill, Pennsylvania, had experienced a reviving:

> There was scarcely an hour's cessation of prayer and praise from the commencement to the close of each of these meet- ings. A "cloud of mercy" gathered about the preachers' tent and poured out its contents about midnight upon the inmates thereof. The following day was a great day for the people.[200]

In 1857 renewal fires fell without any special planning, nor any attempt to organize. One person involved in this move of God said, "This advent was so sudden and heralded, that ministers were in many cases taken by surprise, and scarcely able to realize that awakening . . . (was) breathing on the hearts of their congregations."[201]

In 1857, New York City was transformed as the result of a prayer meeting led by Jeremiah Lanphier. Lanphier was a member of the North Dutch Church in downtown New York at a time when the cities of America were changing rapidly. Downtown districts in cities such as New York were becoming more and more industrialized, and citizens were moving to other locations. Many of the churches moved their congregations out of downtown New York, but the North Dutch Church decided to remain and to draw a new congregation from among the immigrants living around the church. There are two aston- ishing facts about the North Dutch Church that were presented in a new book entitled *The New York City Noon Prayer Meeting*, based on the writings of a man who participated in that great mid–eighteenth century revival: (1) The Old Dutch Church was located in the vicinity where the World Trade Center stood before September 11, 2001— between West Street and Greenwich at the crossing of Fulton Street; and[202] (2) the church was of Dutch origin, with its founders having immigrated from Holland. The church had belonged to a number of Christians who, in the sixteenth century, protested in the strongest and most resolute form against the errors and corruptions of the Roman Catholic Church.[203] Thus, the founders of the North Dutch Church are outstanding examples of the early settlers who came to America to get away from the oppression of the Church in Europe.

In order to reach the people of the city, the North Dutch Church hired Lanphier as a full-time lay evangelist.[204] Lanphier was to personally contact everyone who lived within walking distance of the church to invite them to services. While doing so, he conceived the idea of a noon prayer meeting for businessmen and made preparations for his first prayer meeting to be held on September 23, 1857. Prior to the meeting, he passed out bulletins to everyone that he saw, inviting them to the prayer meeting. On the day of the first prayer meeting, alone in the church, he knelt in prayer with his heart broken for the purposeless despondent masses of New York City.[205] By one o'clock, six people had joined him. The next week, there were twenty. The week after that, there were forty, and those in attendance suggested that they meet every business day. By October 8, there were so many in attendance that they had to move to a larger meeting room. By the fourth Wednesday, there were over one hundred present, many of whom did not profess religious faith, but were under the conviction of sin.[206]

The "Fulton Street meetings" drew so many men and women that the gathering moved around the corner to a larger church. Other churches began to follow suit, opening their churches during the noon hour. "Soon there was such a need for places to pray that police and fire stations opened their doors for prayer."[207]

Lanphier moved his prayer meeting to Burton's Theater in New York City. The first meeting at Burton's was filled to capacity thirty minutes before noon, while hundreds stood in the streets. Within six months, 50,000 were meeting daily in New York, while thousands more prayed in other cities.[208]

Lanphier's prayer meetings continued at Burton's Theater during 1858. On March 20,1858, *The New York Times* commented on the crowd:

> In this city, we have beheld a sight, which not the most enthusiastic fanatic for church observance could ever have hoped to look upon. We have seen in the business quarters of the city, during their busiest hours, assemblies of merchants, clerks, and working men, to the number 5,000, gathering day after day for a simple, solemn worship. Similar assemblies we find in other portions of the city; a theater is turned into a chapel; churches of all sects are open and crowded by day and by night.[209]

The crowds overflowed from the Fulton Street meetings to the churches. On one occasion, a local minister arose during a meeting and announced:

> I was here until three o'clock or so, dealing with men who were seeking Christ as Saviour. There must indeed be many more. So I wish to announce that our church will be opened from tonight onward—indefinitely—for the preaching of the gospel.[210]

Dozens of churches throughout New York City started weeknight meetings for the revival of believers.[211] The Fulton Street prayer meetings went on for a century; J. Edwin Orr reported that he participated in such meetings nearly eighty years after their commencement.[212]

In Canada camp meetings sprung up, drawing 5,000 to 6,000. In April 1858 a Methodist newspaper reported that unusual spiritual awakenings had spread over Canada.[213] While Lanphier was starting his prayer meetings in New York, churches in Philadelphia also began to pray for revival. News of the prayer meetings in New York led to meetings in Jayne's Hall in Philadelphia. The first noon prayer meeting in the city of Philadelphia was held in the Union Church on November 23, 1857. At first, the attendance was far from encouraging, with thirty-six being the highest number present. Even though the numbers were small, the meeting adjourned to the anteroom of the spacious Jayne's Hall, where, as reported by a witness, dramatic changes occurred almost in an instant:

By Monday, March 8th, the attendance in the smaller apartment of the Hall had reached three hundred, and by the next day it was evident that many were going away for want of room. The persons present, with much fear of the result, yet apparently led by Providence, on Tuesday, March 9th, voted to hold the Meeting the next day at twelve o'clock in the large Hall. It was our privilege to be present at that time, Wednesday noon. The Hall has seats for twenty-five hundred people and *it was filled.* The next day it was filled again, with the galleries, and it was obvious there was not room for the people. The curtain was therefore drawn away from before the stage, and that thrown open to the audience. The next day, Friday, the partition between the smaller and the larger rooms was taken down, and the Hall from street to street thrown open.

. . . *three thousand souls at once on one week-day after another, at its busiest hour, bow before God in prayer for the revival of his work.* The men and women, minister and people, of all denominations or of name, all are welcome—all gather.[214]

The description by the witness of this event continues:

> No man there, no man perhaps, living or dead, has ever seen any thing like it. On the day of Pentecost, Peter preached; Luther preached: and Livingston, Wesley, and Whitefield! Great spiritual movements have been usually identified with some eloquent voice. But no name, except the Name that is above every name, is identified with this Meeting. "Yes," said a clergyman, on the following Sabbath, "think of the Prayer Meeting this last week at Jayne's Hall, literally and truly unprecedented and unparalleled in the history of any city or any age; wave after wave pouring in from the closet, from the family, from the Church, from the union prayer meetings, until the great tidal or tenth wave rolled its mighty surge upon us, swallowing up for the time being all separate sects, creeds, denominations, in the one great, glorious and only Church of the Holy Ghost."[215]

The revival in Jayne's Hall of Philadelphia also created national attention. The Jayne's Hall prayer meeting was described in a telegram: "Jayne's Hall daily prayer meeting is crowded, upwards of 3,000 persons being present, who with one mind and heart glorify one Father in Heaven for the mighty work He is doing in our city and country in the building of saints and conversion of sinners."[216]

The Jayne's Hall prayer meeting was considered the "largest prayer meeting ever held in the world," but the facilities soon became too small to hold the large numbers that attended, and the meetings spread to Handel and Hayden Hall and the American Mechanics'

Auditorium.[217] A contemporary reported the expansion of the prayer meetings as follows:

> The lecture room having become too strait for the multitude of worshippers, similar union prayer meetings were established further west and north in the afternoon, and also in the Handel and Hayden Hall at noon, the attendance at the latter place amounting at times to a thousand or twelve hundred persons. Taking all the union prayer meetings together, independent of the regular Church prayer meetings in the evening, the number of those who daily met for prayer about this time was at least FIVE THOUSAND.[218]
>
> Meanwhile the increase of attendance at public worship on the Sabbath, and the number of churches opened for services during the week, was beyond all precedent. During the latter part of the winter, rarely indeed would you pass the lecture room of an evangelical Church in the evening, that was not lighted up for prayer or preaching. Sometimes even the main body of the church itself was not able to accommodate the multitude of worshippers.[219]

By the fall of 1858, large halls in New York City were filled to capacity for prayer meetings. The move of God was so popular that leading secular papers such as *The New York Herald* began to publish "revival extras" to report spiritual happenings from across the nation.[220]

During November, news came of revivals and great numbers of converts in Washington and Iowa, where there was "never such evidence of the mighty power of the Holy Spirit." Revivals were occurring in congregations in San Francisco, Brooklyn, Long Island, Connecticut, and Portland, Maine.[221]

Documents of the period reveal that revival reached every city in the mid-West, including Cincinnati, Cleveland, Louisville, Indianapolis, Detroit, Chicago, and St. Louis. In two months in the state of Ohio, 200 churches recorded 12,000 converts.[222] This 1857–1858 prayer revival seemed to be independent of all human agency, except the prayers of the faithful. In every major city from the Mississippi to the Atlantic, there appeared to be at least one organized daily united prayer meeting, and the number of towns and villages following suit went uncounted. Prayer meetings were organized in numerous business houses. A daily meeting for intercession was conducted in one of the largest printing establishments in New York City. In New Jersey a prayer meeting was organized in the office of one of the officials of the railroad company. Prayer meetings spread through the country where the rural residents organized their own prayer meetings.[223]

Proving that this revival was a sovereign act of God, a ship arrived in New York Harbor whose captain and entire crew of twenty-nine men had been converted in the middle of the Atlantic Ocean. Soon five other ships sailed in, whose captains had been brought to Christ on the open sea.[224] It was reported that there was a definite zone of heavenly influence across the Eastern seaboard. The battleship *North Carolina,* anchored in New York City with more than 1,000 men, became a house of prayer. Four sailors started a prayer meeting on the ship; moved by the Spirit of God, they began to sing. Some of the crewmembers began to mock the young believers, but were soon gripped with conviction for their attitude. Night after night, prayer meetings were held on the battleship, and more hardened sailors were broken in repentance and faith. The *North Carolina* became a revival center serving as a receiving ship for the navy. Crewmen from different ships changed assignment to this ship, as the tide of revival literally swept across the sea.[225]

One businessman attending one of Finney's meetings in Boston reported "I am from Omaha, in Nebraska. On my journey east, I have found a continuous prayer meeting . . . about 2,000 miles in extent." Nationwide, the number of converts reached 50,000 a week and continued for a period of two years at the rate of 10,000 a week.[226] Orr estimates that between 1857 and 1859, out of an American population of 28 million, all mainland denominations experienced conversions exceeding one million souls and perhaps another million who were already members of churches, but not previously meaningfully converted.[227]

Surveying the awakening, Henry Clay Fish, an American Baptist minister and publisher, stated in a religious journal:

> . . . such a time as the present was never known since the days of the apostles: Revivals now cover our land sweeping all before them as upon the day of Pentecost, exciting the earnest and simultaneous cry from thousands . . . Ministers baptized with the Holy Ghost preach with a new power and earnestness, bringing truth home to conscience and life as rarely before. Meetings are held for prayer, exhortation, and conversion with the deepest interest and most astonishing result. Not only are they held in church or from house to house but in great marts of trade and centers of business.[228]

Additional spiritual awakenings spread along the mid-Atlantic states. In Albany, the state capital, early morning prayer meetings led by six state legislators met in the Court of Appeals opposite the senate chambers, and soon overflowed into other rooms of the Capitol.[229]

During the latter part of 1857, many churches in Connecticut and other parts of New England were affected by the move of the Spirit. By spring 1858 the capital city of Providence, Rhode Island, enjoyed a period of revival never seen before, with every church affected by large numbers of conversions and united morning prayer meetings overflowing.[230] In Boston "an increased feeling in favor of temperance has manifest itself with the progress of the revival, producing a visible effect upon the business of the liquor dealers. Some barrooms are almost deserted of customers."[231] Reports came from New Hampshire of ". . . a great prayer revival in almost every city and town and neighborhood . . . daily prayer meetings held at noon in all the cities and large places, not only in the churches, but in halls and stores and other places of business, the voice of prayer everywhere in accordant melody."[232]

In Cincinnati, attendance was so large at daily prayer meetings that meeting places were not available. Businessmen, lawyers, judges, professionals, and clergymen became empowered by prayer to minister in towns and cities within a radius of 150 miles.[233]

Meetings in Detroit, Michigan, overflowed as zealous businessmen of all denominations gathered for prayer. Missouri was no exception, as the *St. Louis News* observed in March of 1858:

We do not remember ever to have observed such a general awakening of the people on the subject of religion as it is percepted throughout the land at this time. There is scarcely a single county in the western states that has not shared in the refreshing blessing. Almost every country meeting house in Missouri has been or now is the scene of earnest, zealous preaching, resulting in revival.[234]

The most informed and reputable Christian organization of the day was the Evangelical Alliance. Its monthly publication, *Evangelical Christendom,* featured a report of the "extraordinary revival in the United States" by a Lutheran professor, who observed:

> The revival that sprang up last year [during 1857] nearly simultaneously all over the country is the most remarkable ever known in the history of the Christian Church. Its origin and cause indicate its genuineness as divine. Thousands upon thousands converted to God have enrolled their names with the Christian Church.

Fifty years later, the *Evangelical Christendom* insisted that the effects of the Great Awakening, which "shook the world," could still be seen.[235]

One of the converts of the layman's prayer revival was Dwight L. Moody. In 1851 one of New England's best-known revivalists, Edward Norris Kirk, minister of the Mount Vernon Church in Boston, started the Young Man's Christian Association (YMCA). In early 1857 Moody attended a YMCA prayer meeting where his life was transformed. Although never ordained as a minister, Moody became a great evangelist. As an example of his dynamic ministry, during a three-month campaign in 1876 in Chicago (which had a population of 400,000), Moody's meetings were attended by 900,000 people with 6,000 converts.[236] Moody created Moody Bible Institute, which has ministered to millions and still continues today.

From the New York prayer meetings, awakenings occurred in the British Isles that planted the seed of revival that was to flame up again at the beginning of the twentieth century.[237]

As the man contemplated the events of the mid-1850s, he lifted his eyes to the Father and said, "Father, I see how you brought one great revival to prepare this nation for independence. You brought a second great revival when the nation seemed to forget its Christian heritage, and you prepared America for the internal and external struggles of the early 1800s. And now, Father, you have brought a great revival to prepare this nation for its great national conflict. I know it is no coincidence that the place of the beginning of this great revival was also at the location of our recent terrorist attack on the World Trade Center."

And the Father spoke and said, "Remember my son, that I control the destiny of nations. Never forget that I have a call on this nation to be one nation under God. I called forth this nation for that purpose long before it was established. When my people were scattered throughout Europe, I heard their cries for deliverance and gave them a new land. When Abraham's children were scattered and persecuted throughout all of the world, I heard their cry for deliverance, and I called forth this nation to play a vital role in my plans for their return to Abraham's land. This nation has always been a nation of destiny. Even before Columbus sailed to the West, I called it forth for that purpose. Continue your journey, and I will unfold my destiny for this land."

Chapter 14

"Your glory, O Israel, lies slain on your heights.
How the mighty have fallen!"

"How the mighty have fallen in battle!
Jonathan lies slain on your heights.
I grieve for you, Jonathan my brother;
you were very dear to me.
Your love for me was wonderful,
more wonderful than that of women.
How the mighty have fallen!
The weapons of war have perished!"
—2 Samuel 1:19, 25–27 (NIV)

(Lamentation of David after the death of Israel's finest, including
Saul and his son, Jonathan, in Israel's "civil war.")

THE BROTHERS' WAR

History is determined by great ideas, great men, and great events.[238] By 1860 the two competing ideals of freedom and sovereignty of the states drove this nation in two irreconcilable directions and ultimately to civil war. Two great men changed the course of the Civil War from what could have been the most divisive to the most uniting event in American history. One of these men was Robert E. Lee—first a traitor when he left the Union ranks to join the Confederates, later a hero of the North and the South. The second was Abraham Lincoln—called an incompetent president by many contemporaries, but now considered to be one of the great apostles of freedom in modern history. Although history would establish Lincoln's national heroism, his contemporaries reviled him; they treated him with contempt, and ultimately he was assassinated. But these two great men were to shape the course of American history through one of the bloodiest civil wars ever recorded.

Lee and Lincoln were by nature men of peace (although Lee was trained as a soldier) and neither sought war or considered it productive. However, events beyond their control were driving this nation toward the most painful type of war—a war between North and South, a war between brothers.

LINCOLN AND FREEDOM

During the mid-1800s, the North developed into an industrial center. Production in the North of all goods, with the exception of cotton, greatly exceeded the production of the South. In 1860 the population of the combined eleven Confederate States was approximately 5.5 million free whites and 3.5 million black slaves. The population of the nineteen Union states was about 19 million, with an added 2.5 million in the border states, which supported the Union. During the Brothers' War, an additional one million immigrants increased Northern superiority.[239]

The South, staggering under the weight of its own slavery system, could only watch as the North grew stronger and stronger. Not only was the South threatened by the numerical and industrial superiority of the North, but three other forces beyond the control of the South were driving this nation nearer and nearer to the brink of war:

(1) The South was losing its political clout. The North controlled the House of Representatives and the presidency because of the disparaty in population as well as the majority of the Senate. As slave-free states were admitted to the Union, Northern political domination increased.

(2) The layman's revival added religious fervor to the moral determination of the North that slavery was inhumane. The South had convinced itself that the slaves were inferior subjects who could not care for themselves and that maintaining slavery was not only moral, but the Christian solution.

(3) America refused to resolve the great moral issue of slavery. In the words of America's moral leader, Abraham Lincoln:

A house divided against itself cannot stand. I believe this government cannot endure half *slave* and half *free.* I do not expect the Union to be *dissolved.* I do not expect the House to *fall.* But I *do* expect it will cease to be divided. It will become *all* one thing, or *all* the other. Either the *opponents* of slavery will arrest the further spread of it, and place it where the public mind shall rest in the belief that it is in course of ultimate extinction; or its *advocates* will push it forward, till it shall become alike lawful in *all* the states, *old* as well as *new, North* as well as *South*.[240]

Therefore, the North and South were about to engage in a holy war; there would be no middle ground. Although Lincoln spoke of a nation that would be all free or permit slavery in every state, this was never to be. The greatest hope of the South was secession. Ultimately, the nation would be free of slavery, or the South would secede from the Union.

How could brothers fight against brothers? No one wanted war. But how could war be avoided? When the Layman's Revival set the conscience of the nation against slavery, war was inevitable. The Southerners were convinced that their economic and social system could not survive without slaves. The reluctant combatants played their inevitable roles, which would end in the most painful of all wars; no one was unaffected. Mary Lincoln, wife of Abe Lincoln, had three brothers who fought for the South; all of them were killed. All of the male relatives of Varina Davis, wife of Confederate President Jefferson Davis, fought for the Union. Senator John J. Crittenden of Kentucky had two sons, both major generals, who served in opposing armies. Robert E. Lee's nephew commanded the Union naval forces on the James River.[241] More American soldiers were killed in this war than in all other American wars combined—more than 600,000. More than twice as many Americans lost their lives in one day at Sharpsburg as those that died in the War of 1812, the Mexican War, and the Spanish-American War combined.[242] Of the one million white males who served in the Confederate Army, there were 300,000 casualties.[243]

The person who played the dominant role in this war may

have been the most reluctant of all participants. Abraham Lincoln was the man of destiny that God raised up to deliver this nation through the most trying years in its arduous history. Without Lincoln's indomitable spirit—his commitment to resolving the slavery issue and his determination that this nation was to be united—the Civil War probably never would have occurred; instead, the nation would have divided into two or more nations. Lincoln was an uncommon man from a common beginning; when asked about his childhood, Lincoln said it could be condensed into one phrase—"the short and simple annals of the poor."[244] He came to manhood as a product of the frontier, infused with the qualities of courage, perseverance, self-confidence, and a determination to order one's own destiny.[245] In Lincoln's case, that determination would set the course of the nation. In 1832, when he unsuccessfully entered politics as a candidate for the state legislature, he declared his ambition to be "truly esteemed of my fellow men, by rendering myself worthy of their esteem."[246] This vision would change. During the defining years of his life and this nation, he set his face like flint, without regard for men's esteem, to lead the nation toward the inevitable war.

In his early years, Lincoln manifested no religious convictions. He did not join a church in Indiana when his parents joined. As a young man, he was repelled by religious emotionalism and bitter sectarianism; he had already become a Skeptic or Deist.[247] A few years later Lincoln was impressed with the poem "Mortality," written by William Knox of Scotland. Its first line, "Oh, why should the spirit of mortal be proud?" appealed to the sense of melancholy and fatalism that often left Lincoln despondent.[248]

Many contemporaries did not consider Lincoln to have the capacity to drive the ship of state during the slavery controversy; he was a man of common origin and a peacemaker who often said,

"Persuade your neighbors to compromise whenever you can."[249] When he became a U.S. Congressman in 1847, he took little part in the reform movements that were sweeping the country. Although he opposed the war with Mexico as an act of aggression, he did not agree with those who opposed the annexation of Texas as a slave state; he concluded that slavery already existed, and that one must be realistic about the slave issue. After he was elected to Congress as an attorney, he represented a slave owner in a suit to retain possession of a slave family who had escaped to the free state of Illinois.[250]

But his life was a life of destiny. As a young man, he read of the Revolutionary War and thought, "there must have been something more than common that those men struggled for."[251] The words of the Declaration of Independence, proclaiming the equality of all men, were written in his heart; he often quoted them in his now-famous speeches. When he came to Washington, one of the first things he saw near the U.S. Capitol was a "sort of Negro livery stable" where "droves of Negroes were collected, temporarily kept, and finally taken to Southern markets, precisely like droves of horses."[252] Although Lincoln was by nature broad-minded, tolerant, and inclined to let things alone if possible, those Negro stables near the Capitol of freedom were, in his words, "mighty offensive."[253]

Lincoln could not avoid the slavery problem; every issue that dealt with the admission of states to the Union or states' rights culminated in a confrontation between the North and South over slavery. By 1858, when he ran for the U.S. Senate, the course of his life was set by his own words when he declared that a nation cannot endure "half slave and half free." Before his inauguration as president, Lincoln had determined that slavery was America's great sin, which must be limited or abolished, and that America must never be allowed to divide into two nations. From that day until his death, the determination and commitment of this uncommon man, combined with the events that were now beyond everyone's control, redefined freedom in this nation.

When Lincoln and other Democrats concluded that their party was controlled by the Southern legislators, they formed the Republican party. Lincoln soon became the champion of the new Republicans. The newspapers of the Democratic Party—the stronger party by far—dismissed Lincoln as "a third rate lawyer," "a nullity," a man who "could not speak good grammar," a "gorilla." Using political arithmetic, Lincoln should have been defeated; but the Democratic Party was so divided between the North and South that Lincoln's election as President became inevitable.[254] And so Abraham Lincoln, a humble, self-taught man with a moral commitment to freedom, became America's new president.

Although Lincoln was a peacemaker, his destiny was to be the moral genius of the nation during the Brothers' War. In early December 1860, after Lincoln's election, James Buchanan proposed a constitutional convention to frame amendments guaranteeing slavery to the South; but the South was already committed into secession. On December 20, South Carolina seceded from the Union. By February 1, 1861, Mississippi, Florida, Alabama, Georgia, Louisiana, and Texas had taken similar action. The secessionists took over Federal forts and arsenals, and replaced them with state flags.[255] While Lincoln was traveling to Washington for his inauguration in February 1861, news came that Jefferson Davis had been elected as president of the Confederacy.[256]

At the beginning of his presidency, Lincoln would compromise, permitting slavery to continue in slave states. He refused to acknowledge the rights of a state to secede from the union. "No State, upon its own mere motion, can lawfully get out of the Union," he asserted.[257] But later, as he viewed the slavery issue, he concluded that slavery must be eradicated. Any hope of avoiding secession on peaceful terms ended when Davis was elected as Confederate president; Davis believed the slave system was a benevolent system because of his personal experiences— his brother Joseph was a planter who did not flog or mistreat his slaves.[258] Until Davis became president, he knew little of the South beyond his own part of Mississippi. He refused to believe stories of cruelty to the slaves and insisted that the blacks were better off as slaves in the South than as tribespeople in Africa.[259] Since the South had convinced itself that slavery was a moral and Christian system, perhaps Davis was the right person to serve as its president.

Davis proclaimed that war was the only Southern solution. In this, he was not alone; Alexander Stephens of Georgia expressed the view of the South:

> Lincoln may bring his 75,000 troops against us. We fight for our homes, our fathers and mothers, our wives, brothers, sisters, sons, and daughters! —We can call out a million people if need be, and when they are cut down, we can call another, and still another, until the last man of the South finds a bloody grave.[260]

But God's man for this nation's days of judgment was Abraham Lincoln. There was another Abraham that God had raised up in an earlier day; God led him out of Ur and planted him and his children in the first land of promise. God gave this first Abraham a vision that his children of the flesh and of the spirit would be the children of promise (see Genesis 12:1–3, 13:14–17, and 16) and revealed His heart as He told him that judgment would come upon his children, but they would remain in His eternal favor (see Genesis 15). Similarly, through this second Abraham, God planted the vision of judgment for the nation's sin, along with God's eternal favor.

Although in younger years Lincoln did not appear to be a religious man, and in later years he shunned organized Christianity, few men in history, by words and action, have demonstrated such a Christian vision. Excerpts from his speeches that show his understanding of God's covenantal relationship with America are contained in an appendix to this book.

In his 1863 proclamation appointing a national day of prayer and fasting, Lincoln stated:

And, insomuch as we know that, by His divine law, nations like individuals are subjected to punishments and chastisement in this world, may we not justly fear that the awful calamity of civil war, which now desolates the land may be but a punishment inflicted upon us for our presumptuous sins to the needful end of our national reformation as a whole people? . . .We have been the recipients of the choicest bounties of Heaven. We have been preserved these many years in peace and prosperity. We have grown in numbers, wealth and power as no other nation has ever grown. . . .But we have forgotten God. We have forgotten the gracious Hand which preserved us in peace, and multiplied and enriched and strengthened us; and we have vainly imagined, in the deceitfulness of our hearts, that all these blessings were produced by some superior wisdom and virtue of our own. . . . Intoxicated with unbroken success, we have become too self-sufficient to feel the necessity of redeeming and preserving grace, too proud to pray to the God that made us! . . . It behooves us then to humble ourselves before the offended Power, to confess our national sins and to pray for clemency and forgiveness. . . . All this being done, in sincerity and truth, let us then rest humbly in the hope authorized by the Divine teachings, that the united cry of the nation will be heard on high and answered with blessing no less than the pardon of our national sins and the restoration of our now divided and suffering country to its former happy condition of unity and peace.[261]

Perhaps above all other purposes, the nineteenth-century Abraham was called by God as a prophet to reveal the Father's heart and eternal purpose for this nation. It may be that words, more than action, win the world. Although Lincoln was despised and reviled by many, his words sustained this nation in its greatest time of trial and planted for future generations a vision of one nation under God, a land of freedom.

LEE AND WAR

The second great man that God used to bring this nation through the Brothers' War was to be the primary instrument in the reconciliation of the North and the South at war's conclusion. Although he was the commander-in-chief of the Confederate Army, at the end of the war both North and South viewed Lee with pride as America's greatest general.

That Lee was alive was a miracle; during the Mexican War, when Lee was returning from reconnaissance, a nervous sentry, fearing that Lee and his companion were Mexicans, fired his pistol at them. The ball passed so closely between Lee's arm and side that it singed his tunic.[262] Later in the same war, while patrolling, Lee hid under a fallen tree from morning until nightfall, in the presence of a Mexican patrol.[263]

Lincoln offered Lee the position of field commander of the Union Army. Lee hated slavery and had never owned a slave; but with a firm belief in the sovereignty of the states and a commitment to his native state of Virginia, he chose to resign from the U.S. Army and join the Confederates. His contempt for slavery was stated in a letter to his wife in which he wrote that "slavery as an institution is a moral and political evil in any country . . . I think, however, a greater evil to the white than to the black race . . ."[264] Most military men would not have refused the offer to be the commander-in-chief of the national army; but Lee chose to be a traitor to his country by joining those who had seceded from the Union with the same moral commitment as the revolutionaries at the time of the Declaration of Independence. He was a man of principle; both the North and the South would come to recognize his moral authority during the long Civil War.

In the early days of the war, defeat appeared inevitable for the Confederacy. There had been early Confederate victories; but on May 31, 1862, when Lee took command of the army of Northern Virginia, Union troops, under the leadership of General George B. McClellan, were entrenched within five miles of the Confederate capital of Richmond, and the Southern army was without organization and discipline. Lee was puzzled when the men refused to work when asked to dig fortifications and construct defenses. Many of the Southerners had never done manual labor; some of the soldiers, even privates, had their servants with them to perform their menial duties. Following the example of George Washington, Lee rode daily along the lines, encouraging the men, who soon began to take pride in his praise and responded to his requests.[265]

Lee is often considered to be one of the four great military men of history, ranking with Julius Caesar, Peter the Great, and Napoleon. Military leaders since the Civil War have studied his

innovative tactics.[266] But above all, Lee was a man of moral commitment, and for that, he was respected by the soldiers of the North and
the South. Throughout the war, when Lee rode by his men, they
would shout "Lee, Lee, Lee, Lee, Lee!" When he rode in view of the
Northern forces, the soldiers often stood at attention and removed
their hats, shouting, "We wish you were ours!" Lee would then tip his
hat in respect. Even though he led the Southern forces in some of the
bloodiest wars in history, he was widely respected as a national hero.[267]

Throughout the Civil War, the Confederate Army, which was
greatly out-manned, depended upon Lee's masterful military leadership. In the early days of the war Lee knew he could rely on two
things about General McClellan: he was extremely cautious and slow
to move, and he was unaware of his vast numerical superiority. Lee's
men skillfully misled McClellan into assuming that the Southern
forces were much greater than they were. Shortly after Lee became
commander, near Norfolk, Confederate Major General John B.
McGruder sent a column of men into the woods and across a road,
in plain view of the Union outposts. For hours McGruder's men circled,
crossing and re-crossing the road, giving the impression to the Union
of a larger body of soldiers.[268] On other occasions Lee's men dragged
items on dirt roads, stirring up the dust, leading McClellan's men to
assume the presence of massive troop movement. At Manassas,
Confederates painted trees black and put them in trenches to give the
appearance of cannons, convincing McClellan that the Confederate
position was impregnable.[269] Because of Southern tactics and inade-
quate reconnaissance, McClellan became obsessed with the notion
that he was outnumbered by a battle-hardened Confederate Army.[270]

Had Lee assumed the Union command when Lincoln offered
it to him, the war would have ended in 1862. Decisive and quick to
act and understanding the importance of reconnaissance, he would

have moved quickly and destroyed the Southern army before it had time to mobilize. His knowledge of the size of the enemy forces and their location was always superior to the Northern commander.

When Lee took command, his first responsibility was to drive McClellan from Richmond. To do this he sent his most trusted warrior, "Stonewall" Jackson, to the North to threaten Washington, D.C., and to draw Union forces north away from Richmond. On the day chosen for battle, Jackson engaged McClellan's forces from the North in a simultaneous assault with the other Confederate forces, starting what is referred to as the Seven Days' Battle. On June 26, 1862, Lee's initiatives began. Within seven days, he had driven McClellan from Virginia. While McClellan retreated, Lee had an opportunity to destroy the general's confused army, and therefore a chance to end the war. But Lee was unable to successfully coordinate his forces, and McClellan escaped. The first great opportunity for a Confederate victory passed with the end of the very costly Seven Days' Battle. Of 85,500 Confederate soldiers at the beginning of the campaign, "3,286 were dead, 15,909 were wounded, and 946 were missing."[271]

The Seven Days' Battle was followed by Confederate victories. Three months to the day after Lee took command of the army of Northern Virginia, the Confederates won the decisive Second Battle of Manassas. When Lee took command, McClellan's troops were entrenched near Richmond. Western Virginia was in the hands of the Union, and the North Carolina coast was occupied by Union troops. Three months later, Union troops had almost completely evacuated West Virginia; they had surrendered the North Carolina coast, and the Federalists were in full retreat to Washington. Officials in the capital had given orders to ship all movable government property to New York.[272]

But Lee could not take comfort in victory. The North was much more populous than the South, and the weakened Northern army would soon be replenished. In fact, Lee learned that 60,000 replacement troops had already been received in Washington. The South could not call up or equip large numbers of troops: uniforms were in rags, thousands of men were shoeless, ammunition was scarce, and the cavalry's horses were exhausted.[273] The weaker side could not wait—it must seize the initiative and move to the North or face inevitable defeat.

Two possibilities for victory existed: the people of the North might lose heart and allow the South to secede, or (a more remote possibility) there might be total victory.[274] The Confederates moved into Maryland. As they marched, observers said that they had never seen an army so filthy, ragged, and ill-prepared. One Federal correspondent wrote in disgust, "Ireland in her worse straits could present no parallel." A boy who watched them march by said, "They were the dirtiest men I ever saw, a most ragged, lean, and hungry set of wolves. Yet there was a dash about them that the Northern men lacked."[275] It was reported that you could smell the Confederate Army before they ever arrived;[276] but Lee had shaped this army into a great military force, which man-for-man could handle all the North had to offer.

Three cigars were actually instrumental in the bloodiest day of the war and may have prevented the Confederate dream of ultimate victory. Lee developed a plan to move into Maryland, block McClellan's railroad supplies, and separate the forces on the East from the West. By doing so, McClellan's diminished and disorganized army would be cut off from supplies and reinforcement. Lee could then destroy McClellan's army. Confident that he could count on McClellan to cautiously take three to four weeks to prepare for war, on September 9 Lee gave written copies of his plans to his officers. One staff officer, whose identity is unknown, wrapped three cigars in his copy of the plan.

On September 13 McClellan unpredictably moved his forces to engage the Confederate Army, shrewdly struck Lee's army at its most vulnerable point, and threatened to divide and possibly destroy it. Only by the skillful maneuvering of Lee and the heroic actions of his men was the Confederate Army able to survive and retreat toward Virginia.[277] But between Lee's army and Virginia was Sharpsburg, which will forever be known as the bloodiest battlefield of the Civil War.

The only question at Sharpsburg was whether the Army of Northern Virginia would survive. On September 17, 1862, over 100,000 men of the North and South engaged in the bloodiest day of the war, with approximately 22,000 casualties. By midday, the Union forces had threatened to break Confederate ranks. At 4:00 PM, 2,000 men of A. P. Hill's division raised a defiant rebel yell, met the Federal advance, and repelled it, saving Lee's army from almost certain destruction. Of 36,000 Confederate infantry engaged in the Battle of Sharpsburg, there were more than 10,000 casualties, out of a total of 13,609 Confederate casualties in the entire Maryland operation. McClellan lost more than 12,000 men at Sharpsburg.[278]

Lee could not understand McClellan's unexpected rapid troop movement, which was so contrary to his normal leadership. Later, he learned that one of McClellan's soldiers had picked up three cigars wrapped in Lee's plans for the Maryland invasion. McClellan had advanced with full knowledge of Lee's position and plans.[279] Tobacco was first harvested by the Indians of North and South America.[280] Prior to the Civil War, Virginia, by use of slave labor, became the primary tobacco-producing state in North America. Ironically, the army of Northern Virginia was almost destroyed by three cigars.

Lee's army returned to Virginia to reorganize. Since McClellan was slow to start his campaign against Lee in Virginia, the Southern troops had time for the four things they needed: rest, food, refitting, and discipline. Under Lee's leadership, the spirit of the army was as high as it had been before Sharpsburg.[281] The greatest shortage was shoes and horses. Throughout the battles, many Southerners were barefooted; the shoes now supplied to some units were strips of untanned hide in the form of moccasins so long that the soldiers could scarcely walk. Because of the shortage of horses, many of the cavalry were committed to traveling by foot.[282]

The Army of Northern Virginia was to fight a Northern army under a new commander. Major General Ambrose E. Burnside became the second of a series of commanders of the Army of the Potomac before Lincoln finally settled on Lee's fellow soldier of the Mexican War, Ulysses S. Grant. Burnside first battled Lee in the streets of Fredericksburg with the most massive army ever displayed to the ragged Southern army.[283] In the battle that followed, Lee continued his mastery over the Northern commanders. The battle ended in a Southern victory, with 12,653 federal soldiers lost, compared to 5,309 Confederate casualties, of which many were trifling wounds.[284]

Other Confederate victories followed, and the Confederate soldiers began to believe themselves invincible; but to the watchful eyes of General Lee, the seeds of potential destruction had been planted. The first evidence of future defeats surfaced when "Stonewall" Jackson was accidentally mortally wounded by his own men. Jackson was Lee's right-hand man; many of Lee's victories occurred as he sent Jackson's troops behind the enemy to disrupt its forces.[285]

There were other signs of problems for Lee: a shortage of horses for the officers, gunners, and cavalry; a shortage of feed for the horses the Confederacy did have; a severe lack of food and supplies for the men; a large death toll of officers in the Confederate victories after Sharpsburg, leaving a shortage of competent leaders; and a large number of general casualties, comparable to that of the Northern army, despite the Southern victories.[286] The North had the manpower to replenish its army, but the South did not.

Since Lee could no longer feed his army in Virginia and Federal forces were moving to Tennessee, North Carolina, Vicksburg, and other areas of Virginia, the necessity arose for a bold and decisive move or the South would not survive. Perhaps if the Confederate Army moved north, the presence of an enemy army on Northern soil might give impetus to the ever-present peace movement of the North.[287] And so circumstances beyond Lee's control once again dictated the course of the war. The Confederate Army was destined to travel north, to a small town in Pennsylvania called Gettysburg and a little hill fatefully named Cemetery Hill.

North they traveled. Lee's immediate destination was Harrisburg, with a plan to cut communication lines of the Northern army between the East and the West.[288] His ultimate destination was Washington, but the battle that would end the Confederates' opportunity for victory took place at Gettysburg.

At Gettysburg, as in Lee's days of reconnaissance in the Mexican War, he looked for a high point from which to control the battle; that point was Cemetery Hill. For three days the battle of Gettysburg raged. On July 1, 1863, the first day of the battle, Lee had the opportunity to take Cemetery Hill, but his new and inexperienced officers and the reluctant old soldier, James Longstreet, did not respond quickly enough to secure victory. Longstreet, who had been the general of the Army of Northern Virginia, was a reluctant participant in all of the Battle of Gettysburg. Repeatedly, at critical moments of the battle when victory was possible, Lee asked the same question, "What can detain Longstreet?"[289] The second day Confederate troops gallantly assaulted Cemetery Hill. That day ended with the federal troops holding on to the hill against Confederate assaults.[290]

During the night of July 2 Union General Gordon Meade met with his corps commander to decide whether the Northern troops should stay and fight or head south to the Baltimore Pike. Their choice to stay determined the outcome of the Battle of Gettysburg and perhaps the Civil War and America's destiny as a united nation.[291] Meanwhile, the Confederates took pride in their accomplishments. On occasion they had engaged a Union Army double their own number and driven them from stronger positions.[292] Because the morale of the army was strong, and Union territory and important artillery positions had been won, Lee determined to stay and fight.[293] Thus, the battle continued for a third and fateful day.

The Confederates' last chance to win the Civil War ended on July 3, 1863. The last main assault by the Confederates took place when General George E. Pickett's Virginian division charged Cemetery Ridge in an effort to control Cemetery Hill. During this assault, all of the Southern commanders and officers were wounded or killed; there were no officers of a higher rank than a colonel to lead the army. Pickett's division ran out of ammunition and had to fight with swords and hands. Virtually leaderless and fighting without weapons, the Confederates finally realized they could not succeed and fell back.[294] The battle of Gettysburg ended.

Lee, gathering with his staff to prepare for retreat, suddenly exclaimed, "I never saw troops behave more magnificently than Pickett's division of Virginians did today in that grand charge upon the enemy." A few moments later in a loud voice he exclaimed, "Too bad! Too bad! Oh, too bad!"[295] Lee could have easily blamed the defeat at Gettysburg on Longstreet, who was too slow to respond, but this was not Lee's nature. Lee, an honorable man, accepted all the blame for the loss in the battle that was to ultimately determine the outcome of the Civil War.

The battle was a devastating loss to the nation. The Union Army suffered the loss of 23,000 killed, wounded, or missing, while the Confederate losses were 28,000. One tree in the line of fire contained 250 bullets. Military experts studied 27,000 muzzle-loading muskets piled up on the battlefield; 24,000 were loaded, one-half with two loads, and many with ten loads, leading the experts to reason that the soldiers lost their heads, loaded, re-loaded, and forgot to fire.[296]

Lee retreated south across the Potomac, never to fight again on Union soil. Circumstances beyond Lee's control led him to Gettysburg, and circumstances beyond his control stood in the way of victory. The Confederates would continue to fight, but victory for the South was not to be. This nation was destined to be one nation under God; a Southern victory leading to secession would have defeated God's plan.

Other news tolled the end of the Confederate cause— Vicksburg surrendered to Grant on July 4, and on July 9, Port Hudson, the last Confederate stronghold on the Mississippi, surrendered to the Union forces.[297]

The Civil War lasted two more years. Suffering in the South was great. President Jefferson Davis had to sell his slaves, his horses, and his carriage to buy food. By December 1864, much of the South was starving. In mid-1864 General William T. Sherman cut a swath across Georgia sixty miles wide, destroying railroads, bridges, crops, cattle, cotton gins, mills, and everything else that could be used in the South's war effort.[298] Major General Phil H. Sheridan led his troops in a wholesale destruction of crops, barns, and livestock in the beautiful Shenandoah Valley, in order to deprive the Confederates of necessary food and foliage for livestock.[299]

Finally on Palm Sunday, April 9, 1865, Lee, dressed in his best uniform, said, ". . . there is nothing left me but to go and see General Grant, and I would rather die a thousand deaths." The two generals met at Appomattox Courthouse. With Grant dressed in "rough garb spattered with mud," each man was carefully clothed for the occasion as he wished to appear for posterity.[300] Grant allowed the Southern officers to keep their side arms and horses and asked Lee if there was anything that he could do for his men. Lee quickly responded that his men were hungry and needed supplies, to which Grant replied, "It is done."

Perhaps at no time in history has a war ended on such conciliatory terms. Lee, labeled a traitor when he joined the Confederate forces, was by the end of the war recognized by North and South as a national hero; and Grant was most gracious in his acceptance of the surrender of the Confederates.

Abraham Lincoln survived the end of the Civil War by only five days. On Good Friday, April 14, 1865, Lincoln and his wife, Mary Todd Lincoln, attended the Ford Theatre. She recalled his last words:

> He said he wanted to visit the Holy Land and see those places hallowed by the footprints of the Saviour. He was saying there was no city he so much desired to see as Jerusalem. And with the words half spoken on his tongue, the bullet of the assassin entered the brain, and the soul of the great and good President was carried by the angels to the New Jerusalem above.[301]

The American Civil War, one of the bloodiest wars in history, remains one of the great events to unite this nation. Undoubtedly this occurred through the moral leadership of Lee and Lincoln.

Immediately after the war, Americans from the North and the South viewed Lee and his moral leadership with pride and respect. Although the slavery issue would continue to divide the nation, the general consensus prevailed in both the North and the South that this nation was one undivided nation. Although Lincoln was reviled and laughed at during his lifetime, his visionary words set the course of American history from that day to the present.

The man pondered these events and lifted his eyes to the Father and said, "Father, I know that you rule in the affairs of men. I see that Lee surrendered on Palm Sunday and that Lincoln was assassinated on Good Friday. I am sure that the dates of these events are no coincidence. I also notice that Lincoln saw the Civil War as a national atonement for the sin of slavery.

"My heart aches as I study the Civil War. I read of Brigadier Lewis Armistead who decided to 'go South.' His good friend, Winfield Scott Hancock, gave him a dinner party. They parted with a handshake and tears. Armistead charged Hancock's troops at Gettysburg and was killed.[302] Other good friends from West Point fought to their deaths on opposite sides. This war seemed inevitable. No one could stop it, and yet it was so devastating. How could this be?"

And the Father replied, "My son, every act has consequences. Nothing is ever done without effect. Acts done in defiance of my laws lead to judgment. And the consequences of rebellious acts are great when done in the name of authority.

"The consequences of acts of rebellion are great when done as the sovereign act of a nation.

"The consequences of acts of rebellion are great when done in a land of freedom by the people of the land in exercise of that freedom.

"The effect of rebellion is great when done in a land that I have chosen as a land of promise.

"*The consequences of acts of rebellion are great in a land that I have called to be my nation. The leaders of this nation claim they can do anything with immunity, and the people blindly follow. And those called as my priests and servants have conspired with them.*

"*But will my priests, my servants, and the leaders of this nation continue to conspire against me? Or could it be that you and my other servants in this land and those who minister before me will choose to determine the destiny of this land of promise? Remember the story of Abraham's children. Continue your journey, my son.*"

Chapter 15

A man has come into the world;
his early years are spent without notice
in the pleasures and activities of childhood . . .
when his manhood begins . . . He is then studied
for the first time . . .

This, if I am not mistaken, is a great error.
We must begin higher up; we must watch the
infant in his mother's arms; we must see
the first images which the external world
casts upon the dark mirror of his mind, the first
occurrences that he witnesses; we must hear the first
words which awaken the sleeping powers of thought,
and stand by his earliest efforts if we would understand
the prejudices, the habits, and the passions which
will rule his life. The entire man is, so to speak, to be seen
in the cradle of the child.

The growth of nations presents something
analogous to this; they all bear some marks
of their origin. The circumstances that accompanied
their birth and contributed to their development
affected the whole term of their being.

America is the only country in which it has been
possible to witness the natural and tranquil growth
of society, and where the influence exercised on the
future condition of states by their origin
is clearly distinguishable.

—Alexis de Tocqueville, *Democracy in America*

BLESSING AND CURSE

The Israelites spent 400 years in Egypt; then the Lord delivered them, and Moses led them out. After their bondage, Moses led them for forty years through the wilderness. When they were preparing to enter the land of promise, Moses gave them God's word. Moses' words to the Israelites conclude with the blessings and curses set out in the twenty-seventh through the thirty-first chapters of Deuteronomy. The history of the Jewish people has confirmed those blessings and curses. Obedience has produced blessings; disobedience has resulted in curses. The history of the Jews can be traced through the consequences of their choices to obey or disobey God.

In America, the Civil War purged this nation of its great sin of slavery. Those who were transported to this nation from Africa to be servants were now free. This new land of promise entered into a new era. But what would the future be? As in the case of the first land of promise, there was now before this new land of promise a blessing and a curse.

At the dedication of the burial grounds at Gettysburg, America's prophet, Abraham Lincoln, planted the vision for the future of his beloved nation. In his speech known simply as the "Gettysburg Address," Lincoln spoke of those on both sides who had fought and died at Gettysburg. He said:

> The world will little note, nor long remember, what we say here, but it can never forget what they did here. It is for us, the living, rather to be dedicated here to the unfinished work, which they have, thus far, so nobly advanced. It is rather for us to be here dedicated to the great task remaining before us—that from these honored dead we take increased devotion

to that cause for which they here gave the last full measure of devotion—that we here highly resolve that these dead shall not have died in vain; that this nation under God shall have a new birth of freedom; and that government of the people, by the people, for the people, shall not perish from earth.[303]

His statement is inaccurate only in one respect—the world will never forget what he said there. In the 268-word "Gettysburg Address," this Abraham demonstrated that the nation's strength must rest in a rededication to those beliefs to which it was committed at its birth. Professor J. Rufus Fears, in his lectures entitled "A History of Freedom," states that the "Gettysburg Address" and Declaration of Independence are the two most important documents of freedom in American history. Lincoln drew from the Declaration of Independence in drafting the "Gettysburg Address." Those two documents, more than any other American documents, have committed this nation to a course of freedom and to the fulfillment of its calling to be one nation under God, a land of freedom governed of the people, by the people, and for the people.

Preceding Lincoln's "Gettysburg Address," Edward Everett, Massachusetts orator, spoke for two hours. The audience expected a similar speech from Lincoln and was appalled when he gave his little speech. Almost without exception, the press reviled him. *The Chicago Times* referred to his speech as "the silly, flat, and dishwatery utterance of the man who has to be pointed out to intelligent foreigners as the President of the United States."[304] Lincoln himself considered the speech to be a failure saying to a friend, "Lamon, that speech won't scour. It is a flat failure, and the people are disappointed." However, Edward Everett was one of the first to recognize the greatness of his speech; he wrote to inform Lincoln that he wished he had said in two hours what Lincoln said in two minutes.[305] Soon, newsmen and others began to read the speech with discernment, and the "Gettysburg Address" grew to become one of the most powerful visionary expressions of liberty and freedom ever recorded in the history of man.

The Civil War ended in a peaceful reconciliation of North and South. This was primarily due to the wisdom of Lee and Grant. Near the end of the war, one of Lee's generals suggested rallying more recruits to the Confederate cause. Lee replied:

> General, you and I as Christian men . . . must consider its effects on the country as a whole. Already it is demoralized by four years of war. If I took your advice, the men . . . would become mere bands of marauders, and the enemy's cavalry would pursue them and overrun many wide sections . . . We would bring on a state of affairs it would take the country years to recover from.[306]

After surrendering to Grant, Lee gave his final order to his army:

> I have determined to avoid the useless sacrifice of those whose past services have endeared them to their countrymen. By the terms of the agreement, officers and men can return to their homes . . . I earnestly pray that a merciful God will extend to you His blessing and protection.[307]

When indicted for treason, a charge that was soon dismissed, he calmly answered an indignant friend:

> I have fought against the people of the North because I believed they were seeking to wrest from the South dearest rights. But I

have never cherished toward them bitter or vindictive feelings, and have never seen the day when I did not pray for them.[308]

Grant intervened on behalf of Lee and other Confederate generals to prevent their arrest as "conspirators." But Confederate President Jefferson Davis, who was less conciliatory than Lee, was incarcerated for two years and then released.[309] The generous spirit of Grant in victory and the dignified acceptance of defeat by Lee set the stage for reconciliation between the North and the South.[310]

There were promising signs of a bright future in the South following the Civil War. During the war, revival swept through the Confederate Army, resulting in an estimated 100,000 conversions in Virginia, Georgia, and among the western troops.[311] Conversions during the Civil War produced ministers, as Confederate officers and soldiers enrolled in seminaries after the war. During the Reconstruction days and thereafter, the South was sustained by veterans who entered the ministry, and by devout farmers and businessmen who returned to rebuild the South. The black church emerged in the South after the war; by 1900 there were 2.7 million church members in a black population of 8.3 million.[312] But there was little meeting of the races, even in their Christian faith. From that day to the present, the Christian church has been one of the most segregated organizations in America.

The spiritual foundation of the nation was shaken in the late nineteenth century by three things: evolution, the scientific study of religion, and the changing pattern of American life.[313] Although he sought in his own writing to reconcile his scientific views with Christianity, Charles Darwin's books *The Origin of Species* and *The Descent of Man* challenged the foundation of the Bible and established a whole new philosophy of life that questioned every tenet of Christianity. The Enlightenment of the eighteenth century had

already fueled an abandonment of Christianity by the scientific community, producing a move toward humanism and secularism. In
addition, American life changed dramatically because the settled
rural life and fixed values of most Americans gave way to a mobile
and urban population. As to the treatment of the blacks, the North
may have won the war, but the South won the peace. There was a
firm Southern resolve to keep the South a "white man's country." The
white South preserved the essence of slavery—a pool of cheap sub-
servient labor without the capital outlays or social obligations
imposed by slavery.[313] Few American whites were willing to accept
blacks as equal; the state government of the South made this inequality
plain. State laws were quickly passed in the South to prevent inter-
marriage of blacks and whites, and laws setting new rules for
vagrancies were established, forcing blacks into servile work.[314]

The Northern abolitionists reacted quickly against the
South's treatment of the blacks through a series of Reconstruction
Acts that imposed rigid rules on voters, excluding whites and enfran-
chising blacks. Blacks, who now made up the majority vote, were
manipulated by Northern "carpetbaggers" and Southern "scalawags."
Since many blacks were illiterate, they were easily manipulated and
victimized. Through this manipulation, these carpetbaggers plunged
their hands into the public treasury. Lincoln's party, the Republicans,
corrupted the Southern legislature and judicial system. Since "Honest
Abe" was not alive to steer the course of the Republican party that he
had helped to create, the party used the Reconstruction Acts to fill its
pockets with what remained of the wealth of the South.[315]

White Southerners tolerated blacks in office, but they bitterly
resented those blacks who showed political intelligence and ability;
their existence disproved the Southern concept that blacks were
incapable of improvement.[316]

Because of the hatred of this new government, the Southerners hit back with force. The Ku Klux Klan, a secret society of vigilantes, was birthed in those Reconstruction years. Whites who despised and feared the blacks fostered a hatred that continues to this day.[317] In addition to the Ku Klux Klan, other secret societies were organized under the names of "The Invincible Empire of the South" and "Knights of the White Camellia." Through these societies, blacks were policed, intimidated, whipped, beaten, and murdered. By 1870 these societies had disbanded, but they continue under one guise or another to this day.[318]

Within a decade Congressional reconstruction was destroyed. When whites regained power, a new society was established in the South in which whites were first-class citizens and blacks were citizens in name only; Americans as a whole did not care.[319] America was a thriving nation, and these blacks, who were the focal point of the Civil War, were now ignored in the great expansion period at the end of the nineteenth century. The North did not seem to care that the blacks now worked for intolerably low wages with inhumane working conditions. Therefore, the blacks shifted from one form of servitude to another. This land of promise now experienced a blessing because these disenfranchised citizens were nominally free, but also a curse because the rights of black people as free men and women were systematically ignored.

While the Northern economy expanded, the economic condition of the South after the war was deplorable. Other factors added to the South's misery. The Sherman and Sheridan raids of 1864 destroyed the economic framework of much of Southern civilization. In areas of devastation, whites swarmed out of the underground to loot planters and kill blacks. No banks were solvent; no shops had much to sell, and few schools were open. But the land of the South was fertile and valuable, and that land would eventually revitalize the Southern economy.[320]

In the late nineteenth century in America, the essence of freedom was also defined by other factors. During the Civil War and the rest of the nineteenth century, the role of agriculture was prominent. Since the Northeast was industrializing at a rapid rate and the population of America was swelling due to immigration, the demand for food increased. The Republican Party chose to provide cheap or free land. The great land rush of the nineteenth century took place.[321]

While many engaged in farming, others were discovering the adaptability of the High Plains for livestock. Ranches took over vast areas for cattle production. The cattle towns grew up at Abilene, Dodge City, Topeka, and other locations along the new railways; thus emerged the cattle drives that glamorize the history of the High Plains. By 1890 these cattle drives were over, but they have been immortalized in paintings and novels. By 1900, the romantic era of the American cowboy went the way of legend and folklore.[322]

With the development of farms and ranches throughout America, the fate of the remaining Native American Indians was determined. Each phase of westward expansion resulted in a battle for the land. Since the Native American Indians did not know how to use the political system and could not match the ruthlessness of the cattlemen who fought with more sophisticated weapons, it was inevitable that they would be driven from their land. By the 1890s the Indians were reduced to six small reservations. The ignoble ending of the Native American Indian resistance took place in December 1890 at Wounded Knee, when 146 defenseless Indians, including forty-four women and sixteen children, were slaughtered.[323]

The Western frontier of the late 1800s was a place of violence. Gunfighting was an integral part of the westward expansion, precipitated in part by laws that permitted citizens to defend to the death their land, cattle, farms, families, and even honor. The spirit of lawlessness produced infamous outlaws such as Billy the Kid, Wild Bill Hickock, and the Dalton Gang, and legendary lawmen such as Bat Masterson and Wyatt Earp.[324]

The development of the High Plains in the late 1800s also produced a blessing and a curse—a blessing because of the prosperous farm and ranch land that was developed and the will and determination of the settlers and cattlemen who developed it; and a curse because of the lawlessness and the treatment of the American Indians.

The last half of the nineteenth century was a time of expansion, immigration, and industrialization. America was outgrowing any other nation of the world. At the beginning of the Civil War, the population of the United States was 31 million; it was 40 million by 1870, 50 million by 1880, 63 million by 1890, and 75 million by 1900. Immigrants came, first from England and Ireland; then from Wales, Ireland, Germany, and Scandinavia; then, at the turn of the century, from Poland, Russia, Greece, Romania, Italy, and other eastern and southern European nations.[325]

Before the Civil War, America was the wealthiest nation in the world, primarily because of its tobacco and cotton exports. By the turn of the twentieth century, America had developed into the greatest industrial and financial nation of the world. At the center of this development, small regional rail lines in the 1820s had changed to massive railroads crisscrossing the nation by 1900. At the same time enterprising Americans developed the nation's great natural resources into both small and massive factories, utilizing the rail system for delivery to other destinations in America and throughout the world. Financial giants and small businessmen emerged throughout the nation, primarily at sites of rich mineral deposits and railroad destination points. For each opportunity there was one or more enterprising American to develop or exploit its potential. Honorable men like Andrew Carnegie, America's first steel tycoon, and J. P. Morgan, America's great financier, became the country's great figures of wealth. For each honorable tycoon, there were many of less honor who sought to exploit investors, laborers, or other businessmen.[326] A concentration of wealth in the hands of a few and exploitation of cheap labor produced a class conflict between businessmen and labor that has continued to this day.

Perhaps the most important development of this nation in the late 1800s took place in America's new monster cities—Chicago and New York. At the beginning of the 1830s, Chicago was a fort surrounded by a few farmhouses, with a population of less than two hundred.[327] By 1887 Chicago's population numbered 800,000. Americans came to Chicago from the East, followed by Irish and Germans; Russians, Jews, and Italians formed the next wave, followed by Greeks and Bulgarians; then Mexicans and African Americans poured in. Small, detached tenement houses without proper sanitation housed five or six families in spaces built for one family.[328] The over-crowded environment produced the protection rackets and highly organized crime syndicates for which Chicago is notorious; but because of the initiative of the immigrants, new small businesses and industries sprang up throughout Chicago and the surrounding area.[329] These small businesses, industries, and the area's rich farmland provided the basis for the great mid-nation wealth we see in America today.

New York City and its famous Ellis Island epitomized the period. To commemorate the century following America's independence and its liberal immigration policy, a French sculptor, Frederic Auguste Bartholdi, fashioned the famous Statue of Liberty, which was placed on a pedestal in the New York harbor. A local Jewish relief worker, Emma Lazarus, wrote the sonnet "The New Colossus" from which the following inscription to the statue was derived:

Give me your tired, your poor,

Your huddled masses yearning to breathe free,

The wretched refuse of your teeming shore.

Send these, the homeless, the tempest-toss'd to me.

I lift my lamp beside the golden door.[330]

Because of persecution in Europe, Jews poured into New York City from Poland, Germany, and Russia.[331] At the time of the American Revolution, there were less than 2,500 Jews in America.[332] By 1872 seventy thousand Jews resided in New York City alone. Violent pogroms in Russia sent thousands of Jews fleeing to America; between 1881 and 1900, an estimated 600,000 Russian and Romanian Jews entered the United States, swelling the Jewish population to over one million.[333] By 1893, over half a million Jews crowded into New York City's lower East Side.[334] By the turn of the century the population density in the Tenth Ward of New York was almost five times that of what would become the notoriously overpopulated Calcutta in the 1960s.[335]

Even though it caused an economic strain on the city and its people, New York received the Jewish population that poured in from places of persecution in Europe. In New York City, these Jewish immigrants were transformed from penniless and frightened new citizens in a strange land into self-confident Americans and producers of wealth. The late nineteenth century produced Jewish doctors, lawyers, and enterprising entrepreneurs and businessmen. The Jewish community also produced large businesses such as Sears Roebuck, Bloomingdale's, Altman Brothers, R. H. Macy, Gimbels, Sterns, and Abraham & Straus. These American Jews accumulated massive wealth that provided the primary financial resources for the Jewish exodus to Israel in the twentieth century.[336]

But New York City also became the image of rich-poor America. The poor constituted the sweating labor that fueled clothing firms and factories as New York City became a city with luxury skyscrapers surrounded by slums.

The nineteenth century ended in America with great anticipation for the new century. America was experiencing wealth and prosperity such as the world had never seen. The bells of freedom rang not only in Philadelphia but also throughout the nation. But there were great disparities in the financial positions of its citizens, and it still remained to be determined whether America would see its vision as one nation under God. In the 1830s, French statesman, historian, and philosopher Alexis de Tocqueville toured America. From 1839 to 1840, he published his work *Democracy in America,* which has been called the most comprehensive and penetrating analysis of the relationship between character and society in America. In this work he reached these conclusions:

Upon my arrival in the United States the religious aspect of the country was the first thing that struck my attention;

In France I had almost always seen the spirit of religion and the spirit of freedom marching in opposite directions. But in America I found they were intimately united and that they reigned in common over the same country.

Religion in America . . . must be regarded as the foremost of the political institutions of that country; for if it does not impart a taste for freedom, it facilitates the use of it.[337]

I sought for the key to the greatness and genius of America in her harbors . . . in her fertile fields and boundless forests; in her rich mines and vast world commerce; in her public school system and institutions of learning. I sought for it in her democratic Congress and in her matchless Constitution.

Not until I went into the churches of America and heard her pulpits flame with righteousness did I understand the secret of her genius and power.

America is great because American is good, and if America ever ceases to be good, America will cease to be great.[338]

If he had traveled the same paths in the 1880s and the 1890s, would he have said the same thing? Would he have seen the same distinctions between America and France? In the midst of such prosperity, was the focus of America still on the things of the Father? By 1900 could America be called a Christian nation?

There were promising signs of a new religious awakening. Although Protestant Christianity suffered a gradual decline in membership and interest during the last decade of the nineteenth century, the Holiness Movement had begun. Following the traditions of Wesley, and led by many Methodist ministers, during the 1880s the Holiness Crusade assumed nationwide proportion.[339] Through the National Holiness Movement, camp meetings were revived.[340] By the end of the nineteenth century, the Holiness groups were well on their way toward developing full-fledged denominations. Twenty-three Holiness denominations emerged within the short period of seven years between 1893 and 1900; never before in the history of a nation were so many church denominations founded in so short a time. The direct result of the Holiness Crusade was a formation of the denomination family known as the Holiness Movement, from which the Pentecostal Movement was to be birthed.[341]

The man lifted his eyes to the Father and said, "I see how the eighteenth century provided the framework for a nation of free men and one nation under God. I see how events in the nineteenth century put this nation to a test to determine whether freedom would endure. But I see how ambivalent and inconclusive the events of the nineteenth century were. What will you share with me about this century in America?"

And the Father replied, "I love this country, and I love its people. You see how I have moved in this land when there were those who responded to my call. You see what happens when the people become engrossed in themselves and the prosperity I have given them. Left to their own devices, nineteenth-century Americans would have determined the path of freedom this nation would travel, but they were not left to devise America's ends. Ultimately, the choices they made will not chart the destiny of this nation. I made a covenant with their forefathers; they may have forgotten it, but I will not.

I gave humans the right to choose, but often I hedge them in so their choices are more limited than they think; often they hedge themselves in by their own rebellion. The right to be free exists only for those who follow my Son and seek to obey me. Those who journey their own paths are not as free as they think. Remember, my son, freedom has its foundations in the cross because freedom is founded in my Son's perfect obedience. Continue your journey and look carefully at this nation's struggle to express freedom and the struggle between the prince of this world and Me for the destiny of this nation."

Chapter 16

"America, America, God shed His grace on thee . . ."
From the very beginning, God did abundantly answer
this nineteenth-century prayer we have sung so often.
And there is really no way to measure how much the grace
of God has poured out on this nation is a direct result of
the obedience and sacrifice of those first Franciscan and
Dominican missionaries, the Jesuit martyrs, and the earliest
generations of nameless Americans who chose the Covenant Way.

. . . Entering into covenant with us, God has called the people of
this country to be "a city set on a hill." And since we have repeatedly
betrayed this covenant, it should hardly come as a surprise that His
dealings with America are now severe. Yet even in the midst of
God's judgment can be seen His mercy, for while He does deal
with His people more strictly than with others, He does not reject
them. When He enters a covenant, it is forever. The promises which
He made to the early comers to His New Israel remain intact
and unmodified, though now a far greater amendment of our
lives is required in order to fulfill our end of the bargain.
—*The Light and the Glory,* Peter Marshall and David Manuel

THE CRISIS OF UNBELIEF

Throughout this book I have addressed the struggle for this nation to fulfill its God-ordained call. The two terms that are used to explain God's purpose for America are "one nation under God" and "God's covenant with America." How these two terms play out in the history of America requires some explanation.

ONE NATION UNDER GOD

In our national documents, our pledge of allegiance, and in public forums we proclaim that America is one nation under God, but few people ever offer an explanation of what that term means. It has become a "feel-good" patriotic expression, often without any thought as to what that expression really means. Most view this expression as a relic of days passed. No thinking person in America would advocate a national church to set the moral code for the nation. Immigrants from Europe came to this country to get away from the oppressive church-states. Our forefathers never had the idea that America was to be populated only with Christians. Before the Revolutionary War, Patrick Henry correctly stated this call for America:

> It cannot be emphasized too strongly or too often that this great nation was founded, not by religionists, but by Christians; not on religions, but on the Gospel of Jesus Christ. For this very reason peoples of other faiths have been afforded asylum, prosperity, and freedom of worship here.[342]

Those who came to America from Europe seeking religious freedom envisioned God's call on this land; they committed their lives to carry out God's divine plan and purpose for America; they viewed it as an expression of their Christian faith as they committed their lives to establish a nation of freedom founded upon Godly principles.

There must never be a time when the morality of America is dictated by national leaders or by the Church; our forefathers would never have tolerated it. All men, women, and children must have the right to choose their beliefs and how those beliefs play out in their lives. The role of the Church is to shape the vision of the nation by its example and the manner in which it presents the biblical truths and principles to the nation. The vision of one nation under God is a call for God's people who believe and trust Him to come before Him in prayer and intercession, that this nation may reflect God's glory. It is centered in a relationship between God and His Church and the commitment of that Church to carry God's glory to the nation. It will be manifested when the Church gets its vision of God's call for the Church and the nation. It will occur on a national level as the Church, by its example, prayer, and intercession, changes the spiritual climate and moral perceptions of the nation. Only then can it be said that this nation is one nation under God.

When we look at America in the last two hundred years, this appears to be hopeless. However, a review of history of revivals reveals how quickly things can change. Chapter 9 of this book tells of the great revival that took place at Rogue County in Kentucky, which was one of the most lawless places in the nation. As a result of the prayer and intercession of Christian leaders and an outpouring of revival, Kentucky was so dramatically changed that soon thereafter it was called by Dr. George A. Baxter during his travels to Kentucky "the most moral place I have ever seen."

At most, there will only be a remnant of believers who will catch this vision of God's call in their life and God's call for the nation, but history reveals what God can do with a remnant. These writings reveal remarkable revivals that occurred in America when only a small remnant cried out to God. On each occasion, God raised up a man or a group to carry His glory to the nation. For the expression "one nation under God" to be meaningful, it must first be planted in the hearts of Christians and by their prayer and intercession planted as the national vision manifested in a return to Christian principles that make "freedom" meaningful in the lives of America's citizens.

AMERICA'S COVENANTAL RELATIONSHIP WITH GOD

Peter Marshall and David Manuel in their book *The Light and the Glory* express their surprise when they saw how consistently our forefathers envisioned the covenantal relationship with God. Many who came had a special vision that this nation was called as a nation of nations, a land of "covenant," a new promised land.

Robert Hunt proclaimed this vision when he knelt on the Virginia Beach and dedicated this nation to God.

The Puritans and Pilgrims who settled in New England "were dedicated to actually living together in obedience to God's laws, under the Lordship of Jesus Christ."[343] The Puritans, more than any other, undertook to establish America as a Christian nation by "giving it a Christianity that worked." Not by words, but by example, they set out to establish a place "where it was still possible to live the life to which Christ had called them."[344]

William Penn established Pennsylvania with a Constitution established on biblical principles.

The vision of America as a new land of promise was proclaimed in the churches and in the town meetings; it was a battle cry of independence; it was the expression of our Declaration of Independence and our Constitution and our Pledge of Allegiance;

it was Lincoln's cry of hope in the Civil War; it was proclaimed as the "manifest destiny" of America to spread from the Atlantic to the Pacific during the expansion days and the days of the Mexican War.

Many of our forefathers firmly believed that America was different because of its "manifest destiny" as a nation of freedom, based on a covenant with God that the nation would endeavor to pursue Godly principles and that God would bless this land. With that dream and vision, our forefathers watched God's divine intervention one time after another. They knew this in their hearts—they saw it in their assemblies. They realized that this nation was different from other nations because it was chosen, called by God to be a "city on a hill"—one nation under God.

After its early days, the American people led by the Church have struggled to understand and trust God's promise; it is even more difficult for them to understand God's plans for the nation. When I started to write I had a vague perception of a call that God has for America to be one nation under God. My journey through the writings of America's history, God's dealing with His people in earlier days, and His prophetic Word spoken to me have convinced me of the following:

(1) God has a special call for America, which has been demonstrated over and over again in its history.

(2) God's covenant with America is a covenant with the Church on behalf of the land. It is a covenant with God's people; the Church is responsible for the moral condition of the nation; the Church must answer to God; the Church must envision that God will manifest His glory in this nation.

(3) God's covenant with our forefathers is similar to the covenant that God made with Abraham, and His covenantal relationship with the Jewish people is the underlying revelation of the Old Testament.

(4) National covenants begin in the heart of God, but those covenants are established by the commitment and obedience of those who see God's plans and purposes and are willing to pursue them. Undoubtedly, God called European nations to carry out His purposes. This is evident because Europe was the "cradle of Christianity." But Europe ignored God's call and sought to enforce Christianity in its own vision, plans, and purposes without acknowledging the Lordship of Jesus Christ, which resulted in the Dark Ages. "For many are called, but few are chosen" (Matthew 22:2–13 NIV). Undoubtedly, other nations were called, but when they did not respond, they were not chosen.

(5) God never forgets a covenant made with individuals on behalf of their nation. This is clearly demonstrated by the return of the Jews to their Promised Land in the mid-twentieth century.

(6) Once a covenant is made, a special relationship is established with God. "To whom much is given, much is expected" is an underlying truth that will play out in the history of the nation. It is not a little thing to be a chosen one; the call will play out in victories or defeats until God's plans are established. God will not abandon His covenant, and the consequences of a national rejection of that covenant may be disastrous.

(7) The commitment of the people seals God's covenant. Commitment involves a decision to do the will of God and to do whatever is envisioned in order to carry out God's divine purposes. Commitment is what really distinguishes God's servants from those who never seek to pursue His plans or purposes.

(8) The commitment of our forefathers is the seed of this nation. Without their commitment this nation would be no different than any other. It was their commitment to God's vision and their lifelong pursuit of God's calling that distinguishes this nation.

America's problem can be summarized in one phrase: we have abandoned our covenant with God.

THREE REVOLUTIONS

In this book I have referred to the three revolutions of the eighteenth century that shaped the history of the world. Each revolution started with a noble purpose; however, the impact of each revolution was dramatically different.

(1) French Revolution. The French Revolution started because of the dire economic condition of the masses of the people; because of a shortage of food, many were facing starvation. In such circumstances, the citizens saw the opulence of the monarchy and the arrogance and oppression of the leaders of the Church and revolted. Their battle cry was equality and brotherhood, but without the fatherhood of God. The French Revolution started with great promise, a sense of common commitment and devotion to liberty. But it soon consumed itself, and the guillotine was a visible symbol of French liberation. In fact, the leaders soon realized that they must keep the guillotines busy to satisfy the obsession of the masses for blood and more blood. The blood from the guillotines literally ran in the streets of Paris, with citizens taking the blood and spreading it on their bodies, basking in the glory of the revolution.

Those who spoke favorably of the king or critically of the revolution faced the threat of the guillotines. Houses were searched; citizens were required to attach to their front doors a notice listing all residents who lived inside; entertaining anyone not on the list might lead to the guillotines. Secreting priests, making speculative fortunes, and associating with the rich or with merchants led to the guillotines. Excitement of the masses was expressed by the barber-surgeon,

Achard, who wrote to his brother in Paris, "Still more heads, and every day more heads fall; what pleasure you would have experienced if, the day before yesterday, you had seen national justice meted out to 209 villains. What majesty; what imposing tone; how completely edifying. How many of these grand fellows have this day bitten the dust . . . what cement for the Republic."[345] Eventually, the revolution consumed many of its own leaders, including its most visible proponent, Robespierre.

The French Revolution has been glamorized throughout France and other nations, including America, as an example of equality and brotherhood and liberation from tyranny. Those who glamorized the French Revolution have overlooked the facts and ignored its implications. A nation that follows the French pattern of revolution will consume itself. A desire for liberty without greater goals and purposes will create an insatiable appetite for more liberty and will destroy everything that gets in its way. This revolution discloses the fallen state of man in a way that is not revealed by any other event that has happened in recent history. It clearly reveals that there is no bottom to how far man can fall in pursuit of his own ends. The French Revolution is one of Satan's greatest hours, for it presents his concept of liberty to the world.

(2) English Revolution. Similar circumstances to those that led to the French Revolution were evident in England during the eighteenth century. However, John Wesley, George Whitefield, and their Holy Club led England in an entirely different direction. Tirelessly preaching throughout England in open-door meetings to up to 50,000 people at one time, Wesley and Whitefield changed the spiritual climate of the nation and gave a vision of hope. This revolution shows what can happen when a few men commit themselves to God's purpose with a vision for the nation. Both Wesley and Whitefield

preached in America during the days of the first Great Awakening and planted a similar vision of hope in America that prepared for its great revolution. In America under the ministry of Wesley and Whitefield: (a) the Methodist and Presbyterian churches were established; (b) Methodist circuit riders emerged, which perpetuated the second Great Awakening; (c) the Holiness movement emerged near the end of the nineteenth century and paved the way for the healing ministry and Pentecostal and charismatic movements that were to profoundly affect the Church and mission field in the twentieth century; and (d) the seed was planted for the great spiritual awakening that is presently occurring in America. The English Revolution, more than any other recent event, shows what God can do when a few men commit themselves to His purpose with a vision for revival and the salvation of the nation.

(3) American Revolution. Some 225 years after its birth as a nation, the American Revolution is still a work in progress. Isolated by two oceans and established on principles of freedom, America has shaped its own destiny. Even after 225 years as a nation, its future is still undetermined. It still has the same vision planted by the Declaration of Independence and the Constitution; its concept of freedom, although undefined, provides an opportunity for America to go the direction it chooses to go. It can follow the way of the French Revolution, with its insatiable appetite for liberty destroying everything that stands in its way; or a remnant may emerge such as happened in England, which will lead this nation to fulfill its destiny as one nation under God.

This struggle for America to define itself extends beyond the nineteenth century and is the subject of much of Book Two. After World War II and the Holocaust, simultaneous with the rebirth of the nation Israel, the Church began to arise as a new force in

American history, led by the Pentecostal-Charismatic streams, new evangelical and healing ministries, and leaders such as Billy Graham. At the beginning of the twentieth century, no one could have anticipated the challenges that would be faced in the twentieth century. Those challenges and the opportunity of the Church to emerge as this nation's great hope are the subjects of the last part of Book Two.

THE FAILURE OF THE CHURCH

The one body that should understand this covenantal relationship between God and America is the Church; and yet in the last 200 years, the American people have forgotten that this nation was established in a covenantal relationship with God because the American Church was strangely silent.

There are two reasons why the American Church has failed to understand and proclaim our national covenant with God, and both are centered in a crisis of unbelief. First and foremost, God's covenantal relationship with His people rests upon God's faithfulness. To understand God's faithfulness requires explicit trust. Despite circumstances that often appear contradictory, one must learn what God has said and believe that He will do as He has spoken. This statement is so simple, and yet, despite the clear signs of God's intervention in the history of this nation and the great national spiritual awakenings, the American Church has struggled to believe that God is true to His Word. More than any other characteristic, a failure to believe that God is faithful describes the American Church in the last 200 years.

For God's covenantal relationship to be meaningful in a nation, there must be an obedient response to God's promises; this is the second crisis of unbelief. The American Church, content to rest in its comfortable pews, has not committed itself to diligently pursue God's plan for America; therefore, the Church has no standing to call upon national leaders and American citizens to carry out God's destiny for this nation.

Despite clear signs of the hand of God, this nation, led by its Church, has wavered and turned from the One who created it, relying on its own devices. By the end of the nineteenth century there was no clear vision of God's plans for this nation, and its future was uncertain. One thing was clear—the Church in America, which should have understood God's covenantal relationship with America better than any other group, was strangely silent. Had the American Church lived and proclaimed God's covenantal relationship with America, the nineteenth and twentieth centuries in America would have been dramatically different; but the Church was strangely silent. Had the American Church undertaken to heal the wounds of slavery and racial division after the Civil War, the history of this nation would have been different; but the Church was strangely silent.

Slavery, the Civil War, and the emancipation of the slaves were painful times for America, but they pale in comparison with the events that occurred in the twentieth century. The fingerprints of the Church were firmly imprinted on two great world wars, a devastating worldwide depression, and the Holocaust, which shook the whole world and the foundation of the Christian faith. These events were so devastating, and the failure of the Church to provide answers was so apparent, that mid–twentieth-century Americans were proclaiming that God is dead; even Christian leaders were declaring that the world was in a "post-Christian era."

AMERICA'S JUDGMENT OR GOD'S GRACE

God told the prophet Amos to raise a plumb line over the nation Israel:

> *This is what he showed me: The Lord was standing by a wall that had been built true to plumb, with a plumb line in his hand. And the Lord asked me, "What do you see, Amos?"*
>
> *"A plumb line," I replied. Then the Lord said, "Look, I am setting a plumb line among my people Israel; I will spare them no longer.*
>
> *"The high places of Isaac will be destroyed and the sanctuaries of Israel will be ruined; with my sword I will rise against the house of Jeroboam."*
>
> —Amos 7:7–9 NIV

A plumb line measures the wall to determine whether the wall is straight or whether it is crooked; the crooked walls of a nation will not stand.

The prophet Joel describes unbelievable desolation for his nation:

> *What the locust swarm has left the great locusts have eaten; what the great locusts have left the young locusts have eaten; what the young locusts have left other locusts have eaten.*
>
> —Joel 1:4 NIV

Joel laments the devastation that came upon his nation and its invasion by another nation.

God's call upon the people is described in Joel:

Blow the trumpet in Zion, declare a holy fast, call a sacred assembly. Gather the people, consecrate the assembly; bring together the elders, gather the children, those nursing at the breast. Let the bridegroom leave his room and the bride her chamber. Let the priests, who minister before the Lord, weep between the temple porch and the altar. Let them say, "Spare your people, O Lord. Do not make your inheritance an object of scorn, a byword among the nations." Why should they say among the peoples, "Where is their God?"

Then the Lord will be jealous for his land and take pity on his people.

—Joel 2:15–18 NIV

The rest of the book of Joel describes God's favor—how He drove the armies from the land and restored the nation. It also points to future generations, which usher in the day of Pentecost and the birth of the Church. (Joel 3:18–21)

America is ripe for judgment. This was evident at the end of the nineteenth century, but more apparent at the end of the twentieth century. God must be offended with the Church and the nation—how the Church turned from Him, how the nation has rebelled. Even though there is every reason for judgment in this land and has been for many years, God has withheld His hand of judgment. It must be difficult for Him to witness a nation that He has chosen for a special purpose reject Him. Not only has rejection of God taken place in the high places of the land, but in the assembly of His people. God must ask, *"How can they turn from me? How can they forget their calling? How can they ignore the vision of their fathers? Will they ever learn who rules over the nations? Who raises up and puts down?"* But God must have been patient for a cause in this land, and God's patience and long suffering is what holds the balance in this nation. The next book, which is subtitled *A Dawn of a New Day*, describes the turning of this nation away from God in the twentieth century. It also describes a revitalized Church, which began to emerge from the devastation of the First and Second World Wars and the Holocaust, and a praying Church that began to emerge in the 1990s.

God is patient for a cause.

The history of revivals reveals that God hears those who pray; He sees those who intercede on behalf of the land; He will give them time to come before Him on behalf of the nation. How long? Only God knows. He will wait to see if they are genuine, to see if they are serious, to see if they will continue to come before Him on behalf of the land. Will those who come before God, interceding on behalf of this nation, pray only for a moment? This is what we have seen in prior revivals, which were so short-lived. Or will the prayers of God's people mobilize watchmen to come before God in behalf of the land?

There are encouraging signs of a worldwide groundswell of prayer similar to what has preceded other revivals. Church statisticians have estimated that, at the beginning of the twenty-first century, there were approximately 200 million people worldwide with some degree of commitment to intercessory prayer for the nations and their people. Never in the history of man has there been such a massive prayer movement as seen at the present time.

It is apparent that there is a call on this nation, but God first looks to His people. It is God's people who must come before Him on behalf of the land; it is God's people who hold the future; it is God's people who withhold judgment. How long do we have? How much time has God given us? Will the bowls of judgment pour forth on this land? Or will the praise, worship, and intercession of God's people come before God like incense and pour forth mercy and grace and salvation on America?

And the man lifted his eyes to Heaven and said, "Tell me more of what you will do in this nation."

"My Son came as a priest over the earth. When He was rejected and crucified, He came to Heaven, where He will remain for a time seated at my right hand as the Great High Priest in Heaven. A covenant such as I have made with this land can only be sustained and perpetuated by the priests—those who weep before me in the temple; those who have a passion for my glory; those who minister before me on behalf of the land and its people. Only they can deliver this nation.

"I love America. I have always loved it, even when it was only a thought in my mind before the day of creation. I called those from other lands to plant my principles of truth and freedom in this land. I brought them here in a covenantal relationship with me that they might establish a land of freedom like no other to provide the possibility in a national setting for my glory to be demonstrated.

"This nation faces difficult times because it turned away from me. One cannot turn from the source of life and protection and fail to experience the wrath of the prince of this earth. All life, protection, and provision are in my Son. Those who reject my Son reject that life, protection, and provision. This nation must define itself. It must decide between my Son and the prince of this world as to who will be the Lord over this land. That is the only choice they have. It is a choice that must first be made by my people, for they are the ones who must raise up a standard over this land; they must grasp my call for this land; they must make the choice to follow me and to rest in my Son or turn this land over to the prince of earth. As you see, they have not made the choice because they do not even see the vision.

"Before a nation can make a choice, my people must diligently pursue my plans and purposes and calling—they must make a covenant with me. Once my people make that covenant to follow me, because my

Word is true and my promises are certain, they can change nations—by the power of my Spirit, by the accomplished work of my Son on the cross, by prayer, devotion, and dedication. Ultimately, there must be a national decision that I have really made a covenant with this land. That decision will never involve all of the people. It will always involve only a remnant, but a remnant of my people dedicated to me by prayer and perseverance can change the spiritual climate of the land.

"First, there must be an opportunity to choose to follow me as a national expression. This can never happen until the spiritual forces over the places of government are dethroned; then, and only then, can national leaders make a choice.

"Second, from the highest offices of this land, there must be a declaration and decree that my Son is the Lord over this nation, that this nation is a land of covenant with me, that this nation is one nation under God, and that I am faithful to accomplish what I have started.

"Until this national expression of the Lordship of my Son is made, this nation will experience difficult and painful times, more difficult and painful than they can now envision."

Appendix A

The visionary words of Abraham Lincoln were so important that they deserve special treatment. Therefore, this appendix includes excerpts of many speeches and letters of Lincoln. These writings and speeches reveal that he understood the covenant relationship between God and the United States. He also understood that he was a man called by God for that moment in history. The following are taken from a compilation by William J. Federer, entitled *America's God and Country Encyclopedia of Quotations,* pages 380-391.

In 1862, Lincoln related to a friend, J. A. Reed:

But I am conscious every moment that all I am and all I have is subject to the control of a Higher Power, and that Power can use me or not use me in any manner, and at any time, as in His wisdom and might may be pleasing to Him.

In his speech to the Presbyterians of Baltimore in 1863:

I have often wished that I was a more devout man than I am. Nevertheless, amid the greatest difficulties of my Administration, when I could not see any other resort, I would place my whole reliance in God, knowing that all would go well, and that He would decide for the right.

In answer to a question of L. E. Crittenden, Register of the Treasury: "I am satisfied that when the Almighty wants me to do or not to do a particular thing, He finds a way of letting me know it. I am confident that it is His design to restore the Union. He will do it in his own good time."

Lincoln knew that God was directing his course: "I have always taken Counsel of Him, and referred to Him my plans, and have never adopted a course of proceeding without being assured, as far as I could be, of His approbation."

When Lee's army moved into Pennsylvania and panic took hold of Washington, D.C., Lincoln related his response, as follows: "When everyone seemed panic-stricken . . . I went to my room . . . and got down on my knees before Almighty God and prayed . . . Soon a sweet comfort crept into my soul that God Almighty had taken the whole business into His own hands . . . "

In July 1861, after a Union defeat at the Battle of Bull Run, Lincoln declared a national day of prayer:

And whereas when our own beloved country, once, by the blessings of God, united, prosperous and happy, is now afflicted with faction and civil war, it is peculiarly fit for us to recognize the hand of God in this terrible visitation, and in sorrowful remembrance of our own faults and crimes as a nation and as individuals, to humble ourselves before Him and to pray for His mercy . . . that the inestimable boon of civil and religious liberty, earned under His guidance and blessing by the labors and sufferings of our fathers, may be restored.

In September 1862, after the Union lost the second Battle of
Bull Run, Lincoln wrote his Meditation on the Divine Will:

> The will of God prevails. In great contests each party claims
> to act in accordance with the will of God. Both may be, and
> one must be wrong. God can not be for and against the
> same thing at the same time. In the present civil war it is
> quite possible that God's purpose is something different
> from the purpose of either party—and yet the human
> instrumentalities, working just as they do, are of the best
> adaptation to effect His purpose.
>
> I am almost ready to say this is probably true—that God
> wills this contest, and wills that it shall not end yet. By his
> mere quiet power, on the minds of the now contestants, He
> could have either saved or destroyed the Union without a
> human contest. Yet the contest began. And having begun
> He could give the final victory to either side any day. Yet
> the contest proceeds.

In his second inaugural address in 1865, forty-five days
before his assassination and approximately fifty days before the end
of the war:

> . . . The Almighty has His own purposes. "Woe unto the
> world because of offenses; for it must needs be that offenses
> come, but woe to that man by whom the offense cometh."
>
> If we shall suppose that American slavery is one of those
> offenses which, in the providence of God, must needs come,
> but which, having continued through His appointed time,
> He now wills to remove, and that He gives to both North

and South this terrible war as the woe due to those by whom the offense came, shall we discern therein any departure from those divine attributes which the believers in a living God always ascribe to Him?

In the same address, he spoke of his vision for the nation:

With malice toward none, with charity for all, with firmness in the right, as God gives us to see the right, let us strive on to finish the work we are in, to bind up the nation's wounds, to care for him who shall have borne the battle, and for his widow, and his orphan—to do all which may achieve and cherish a just and lasting peace among ourselves and with all nations.

In 1865, shortly before Lee's surrender, in visiting with State Senator James Shovel of New Jersey:

Young man, if God gives me four years more to rule this country, I believe it will become what it ought to be—what its Divine Author intended it to be—no longer one vast plantation for breeding human beings for the purpose of lust and bondage. But it will become a new Valley of Jehoshaphat, where all the nations of the earth will assemble together under one flag, worshipping a common God, and they will celebrate the resurrection of human freedom.

Endnotes

1. Francis A. Schaeffer, *The Complete Works of Francis A. Schaeffer, A Christian Worldview*, vol. 5 (Westchester: Crossway Books, 1984), 218.
2. Schaeffer, 218.
3. Schaeffer, 219.
4. William J. Federer, *America's God and Country* (Coppell: FAME Publishing, Inc., 1994, now Amerisearch, Inc., 1996), 113.
5. The term "true believers" as used in my text refers to those who seek to follow the teachings of Jesus as demonstrated by the early Church.
6. The term "infidels" refers both to those who did not believe in Christian doctrine and also to those who expressed and practiced a faith different than the teaching of the established Church.
7. H. G. Wells, *The Outline of History*, vol. 2 (Garden City: Garden City Books, 1961), 534–535.
8. Wells, 537.
9. Paul Johnson, *A History of Christianity* (New York: Simon & Schuster, 1995), 252.
10. Johnson, 191.
11. Wells, 548.
12. Johnson, 215–217.
13. George Grant, *The Last Crusader* (Wheaton: Crossway Books, 1992), 32.
14. Grant, 66–67.
15. Peter Marshall and David Manuel, *The Light and the Glory* (Old Tappan: Fleming H. Revell Company, 1977), 31–33.

16. John A. Crow, *The Epic of Latin America* (Berkeley: University of California Press, 1992), 65.
17. Marshall and Manuel, *The Light*, 36.
18. Marshall and Manuel, *The Light*, 31.
19. Marshall and Manuel, *The Light*, 38–39.
20. Marshall and Manuel, *The Light*, 40.
21. Marshall and Manuel, *The Light*, 44–45.
22. Marshall and Manuel, *The Light*, 57.
23. Marshall and Manuel, *The Light*, 58.
24. Marshall and Manuel, *The Light*, 58–59.
25. Marshall and Manuel, *The Light*, 62.
26. Marshall and Manuel *The Light*, 62–65.
27. Crow, 67–68.
28. Crow, 68–69.
29. Crow, 64, 69.
30. Johnson, 7.
31. Marshall and Manuel, *The Light*, 73.
32. Crow, 323–324.
33. Marshall and Manuel, *The Light*, 68–72.
34. Marshall and Manuel, *The Light*, 73–78.
35. Marshall and Manuel, *The Light*, 80–105.
36. Marshall and Manuel, *The Light*, 106–121.
37. Marshall and Manuel, *The Light*, 129–134.
38. Marshall and Manuel, *The Light*, 145–169.
39. Federer, 686.
40. Darrell Fields, *The Seed of a Nation* (Mechanicsburg: Covenant Press, 2000), 24–25.
41. Fields, 35–38, 43.
42. Fields, 47–48.
43. Arnold A. Dallimore andGeorge Whitefield, *The Life and Times of the Great Evangelist of the Eighteenth-Century Revival*, vol. I (Edinburgh: The Banner of Truth Trust, 1989), 413.
44. Dallimore, vol. 1, 413–418.
45. Joseph Tracy, *The Great Awakening: A History of the Revival of Religion in the time of Edwards and Whitefield* (Edinburgh: The Banner of Truth Trust, 1997), 7.
46. Tracy, 8, 10.

47. Tracy, 12.

48. Tracy, 13.

49. Tracy, 13–14.

50. Malcolm McDow and Alvin L. Reid, *Firefall: How God Has Shaped History Through Revivals* (Nashville: Broadman & Holman, 1997), 213–214.

51. Dallimore, vol. I, 426.

52. Marshall and Manuel, *The Light,* 247.

53. Dallimore, vol. I, 263–264.

54. Dallimore, vol. I, 429.

55. Dallimore, vol. I, 432.

56. Dallimore, vol. I, 540–541.

57. Dallimore, vol. I, 541.

58. McDow and Reid, 218.

59. Dallimore, vol. I, 431, 531.

60. Dallimore, vol. I, 544.

61. Dallimore, vol. I, 562.

62. Arnold A. Dallimore, *George Whitefield: The Life and Times of the Great Evangelist of the Eighteenth-Century Revival,* vol. II (Westchester: Crossway Books, 1983), 179–180.

63. Marshall and Manuel, *The Light,* 251.

64. Tracy, 392.

65. Federer, 289.

66. Federer, 288.

67. Marshall and Manuel, *The Light,* 261–266.

68. Marshall and Manuel, *The Light,* 270–276.

69. Federer, 636–637.

70. Federer, 637.

71. Marshall and Manuel, *The Light,* 284–289.

72. Marshall and Manuel, *The Light,* 297–300.

73. Marshall and Manuel, *The Light,* 311–315.

74. Marshall and Manuel *The Light,* 319–326.

75. Federer, 647.

76. Marshall and Manuel, *The Light,* 339–340.

77. Marshall and Manuel, *The Light,* 340–343.

78. Marshall and Manuel, *The Light,* 343.

79. Sir Winston S. Churchill, *The Great Republic* (New York: Random House, 1999), 92.

80. Peter Marshall and David Manuel, *From Sea to Shining Sea* (Old Tappan: Fleming H. Revell Company, 1986), 9–11.

81. Johnson, 68.

82. McDow and Reid, 183–184.

83. Johnson, 356.

84. J. Edwin Orr, *The Eager Feet: Evangelical Awakenings 1770–1830* (Chicago: Moody Press, 1975), 2.

85. Orr, 1–2.

86. Orr, 2.

87. Orr, 3.

88. Orr, 4–5.

89. Orr, 6.

90. Orr, 8–9.

91. Orr, 8–10.

92. Marshall and Manuel, *From Sea,* 93–100.

93. Marshall and Manuel, *From Sea,* 30.

94. Dallimore, vol. I, 19–21.

95. McDow and Reid, 229.

96. Orr, 13.

97. Orr, 14–15.

98. Orr, 19, 29, 32–50.

99. Orr, 51.

100. McDow and Reid, 232–233.

101. Orr, 52.

102. Marshall and Manuel, *From Sea,* 54–55.

103. McDow and Reid, 234.

104. Marshall and Manuel, *From Sea,* 61.

105. Marshall and Manuel, *From Sea,* 61–62.

106. Marshall and Manuel, *From Sea,* 62–63.

107. Orr, 61.

108. Marshall and Manuel, *From Sea,* 235–236.

109. Orr, 61.

110. Orr, 63.

111. Orr, 65–68.

112. Orr, 68.

113. Orr, 69.

114. McDow and Reid, 228.

115. McDow and Reid, 229.

116. McDow and Reid, 230.

117. McDow and Reid, 231.

118. McDow and Reid, 237.

119. Marshall and Manuel, *From Sea,* 75–78.

120. Marshall and Manuel, *From Sea,* 85–89.

121. McDow and Reid, 239–241.

122. McDow and Reid, 240–241.

123. McDow and Reid, 241; Marshall and Manuel, *From Sea,* 310.

124. Marshall and Manuel, *From Sea,* 315.

125. Orr, 199.

126. Federer, 417.

127. Marshall and Manuel, *From Sea,* 197.

128. Marshall and Manuel, *From Sea,* 196–199.

129. Marshall and Manuel, *From Sea,* 197.

130. Marshall and Manuel, *From Sea,* 198–201.

131. Johnson, 238.

132. Johnson, 238–239.

133. Daniel J. Boorstin, *An American Primer* (Chicago: The University of Chicago Press, 1966), 239.

134. Johnson, 317; Marshall and Manuel, *From Sea,* 225.

135. Johnson, 316.

136. Marshall and Manuel, *From Sea,* 225.

137. Marshall and Manuel, *From Sea,* 220–227, 266–268.

138. James Truslow Adams, *The March of Democracy, A History of the United States,* vol. II, (New York: Charles Scribner's Sons, 1933), 1.

139. Marshall and Manuel, *From Sea,* 125.

140. Adams, 72.

141. Marshall and Manuel, *From Sea,* 132.

142. Marshall and Manuel, *From Sea,* 126.

143. Marshall and Manuel, *From Sea,* 145; Adams, 92–93.

144. Marshall and Manuel, *From Sea,* 130–131.

145. Adams, 94.

146. Marshall and Manuel, *From Sea,* 149–157.

147. Marshall and Manuel, *From Sea,* 157–159.

148. Marshall and Manuel, *From Sea,* 166–168.

149. Peter Marshall and David Manuel, *Sounding Forth The Trumpet* (Grand Rapids: Fleming H. Revell, 1977), 163–164.

150. Marshall and Manuel, *Sounding Forth,* 172.

151. Marshall and Manuel, *Sounding Forth,* 177.

152. Marshall and Manuel, *Sounding Forth,* 188.

153. Johnson, 252.

154. Marshall and Manuel, *Sounding Forth,* 164.

155. Marshall and Manuel, *From Sea,* 319–350.

156. Richard Twiss, *One Church Many Tribes* (Ventura: Regal Books, 2000), 38–39.

157. Twiss, 39.

158. Johnson, 373.

159. Marshall and Manuel, *From Sea,* 356–359.

160. From the song "Remember the Alamo" by Jane Bowers.

161. Marshall and Manuel, *From Sea,* 363.

162. Marshall and Manuel, *From Sea,* 363–66.

163. Johnson, 374.

164. Marshall and Manuel, *Sounding Forth,* 128.

165. Johnson, 378.

166. Marshall and Manuel, *Sounding Forth,* 126, 144–156.

167. Marshall and Manuel, *Sounding Forth,* 183–184.

168. Douglas Southall Freeman, *R.E. Lee: A Biography,* vol. I (New York: Charles Scribner's Sons, 1936), 239–240.

169. Marshall and Manuel, *Sounding Forth,* 194–233.

170. Marshall and Manuel, *Sounding Forth,* 166.

171. Johnson, 4.

172. Johnson, 26–28.

173. Marshall and Manuel, *From Sea,* 229–235.

174. Marshall and Manuel, *From Sea,* 260.

175. Marshall and Manuel, *From Sea,* 260.

176. Marshall and Manuel, *From Sea,* 380.

177. Marshall and Manuel, *Sounding Forth,* 289–290.

178. Marshall and Manuel, *Sounding Forth,* 271.

179. Marshall and Manuel, *From Sea,* 262.

180. Marshall and Manuel, *From Sea,* 262.

181. Marshall and Manuel, *From Sea,* 263–264.
182. Marshall and Manuel, *From Sea,* 258.
183. Marshall and Manuel, *From Sea,* 382–384.
184. Marshall and Manuel, *From Sea,* 252–253.
185. Johnson, 891–892.
186. McDow and Reid, 252.
187. Orr, 7.
188. Orr, 6.
189. Orr, 8.
190. Marshall and Manuel, *Sounding Forth,* 425.
191. Marshall and Manuel, *Sounding Forth,* 426.
192. Orr, 14.
193. Marshall and Manuel, *Sounding Forth,* 426.
194. McDow and Reid, 253.
195. Orr, 48–52.
196. Orr, 40.
197. Orr, 40–42.
198. Marshall and Manuel, *Sounding Forth,* 422.
199. Marshall and Manuel, *Sounding Forth,* 423.
200. Orr, 57–58.
201. McDow and Reid, 254.
202. Talbot W. Chambers, *The New York City Noon Prayer Meeting* (Colorado Springs: Wagner Publications, 2002), 18–19.
203. Chambers, 25.
204. Marshall and Manuel, *Sounding Forth,* 417.
205. McDow and Reid, 251.
206. Marshall and Manuel, *Sounding Forth,* 418.
207. Marshall and Manuel, *Sounding Forth,* 419.
208. McDow and Reid, 258–259.
209. Orr, 72.
210. Orr, 73.
211. Orr, 73.
212. Orr, 281.
213. McDow and Reid, 255.
214. Chambers, 110–111.
215. Chambers, 111–112.

216. J. Edwin Orr, *The Event of the Century* (Wheaton: International Awakening Press, 1989), 83.
217. Orr, *The Event*, 84.
218. Chambers, 113.
219. Chambers, 114.
220. McDow and Reid, 260–261.
221. Orr, *The Event*, 58–59.
222. McDow and Reid, 261.
223. Orr, *The Event*, 280.
224. Marshall and Manuel, *Sounding Forth*, 423–424.
225. McDow and Reid, 262.
226. Marshall and Manuel, *Sounding Forth*, 428.
227. Orr, *The Event*, 319.
228. Orr, *The Event*, 77–78.
229. Orr, *The Event*, 94.
230. Orr, *The Event*, 106–107.
231. Orr, *The Event*, 111.
232. Orr, *The Event*, 116.
233. Orr, *The Event*, 124.
234. Orr, *The Event*, 143.
235. Orr, *The Event*, 332.
236. McDow and Reid, 265–266.
237. McDow and Reid, 268–269.
238. J. Rufus Fears, "A History of Freedom" ("The Great Courses" produced by The Teaching Company).
239. Johnson, 462.
240. Johnson, 443.
241. Johnson, 459.
242. Bill Bright and John N. Damoose, *Red Sky in Morning* (Orlando: New Life Publications, 1998), 79–80.
243. Johnson, 462.
244. Benjamin P. Thomas, *Abraham Lincoln* (New York: Barnes & Noble Books, 1994), 4.
245. Thomas, 21.
246. Thomas, 29
247. Thomas, 68.
248. Thomas, 110.

249. Samuel Eliot Morison, *The Oxford History of the American People* (New York: Oxford University Press, 1965), 436.
250. Thomas, 111–112.
251. Thomas, 115.
252. Thomas, 115.
253. Morison, 439.
254. Morison, 446–449.
255. Thomas, 228–229.
256. Thomas, 240–241.
257. Thomas, 246.
258. Morison, 451.
259. Morison, 452.
260. Thomas, 259.
261. Federer, 383–384.
262. Marshall and Manuel, *Sounding Forth*, 205–206.
263. Douglas Southall Freeman, *R. E. Lee,* vol. II (New York: Charles Scribner's Sons, 1936), 239–240.
264. Federer, 363–364.
265. Freeman, *Lee,* vol. II, 86–87.
266. Fears.
267. Fears.
268. Freeman, *Lee,* vol. II, 8.
269. Thomas, 308.
270. Thomas, 286.
271. Freeman, *Lee,* vol. II, 230–231.
272. Freeman, *Lee,* vol. II, 343.
273. Freeman, *Lee,* vol. II, 350–352.
274. Freeman, *Lee,* vol. II, 360–361.
275. Freeman, *Lee,* vol. II, 355.
276. Fears
277. Freeman, *Lee,* vol. II, 359–372.
278. Freeman, *Lee,* vol. II, 398–402.
279. Freeman, *Lee,* vol. II, 410.
280. *Encyclopedia Britannica,* "Tobacco."
281. Freeman, *Lee,* vol. II, 415.
282. Freeman, *Lee,* vol. II, 416–417.
283. Freeman, *Lee,* vol. II, 456.

284. Freeman, *Lee,* vol. II, 471.

285. Freeman, *Lee,* vol. II, 561–563.

286. Freeman, *Lee,* vol. II, 491–496.

287. Douglas Southall Freeman, *R. E. Lee,* vol. III (New York: Charles Scribner's Sons, 1936), 18–19.

288. Freeman, *Lee,* vol. II, 58.

289. Freeman, *Lee,* vol. II, 86–106.

290. Craig L. Symonds, *Gettysburg, A Battlefield Atlas* (Baltimore: The Nautical & Aviation Publishing Company of America, 1999), 59.

291. Symonds, 62.

292. Symonds, 63.

293. Freeman, *Lee,* vol. II, 105.

294. Symonds, 73.

295. Freeman, *Lee,* vol. II, 133–134.

296. Carl Sandburg, *Abraham Lincoln, The War Years – II,* vol. 4 (New York: Charles Scribner's Sons, 1939), 342.

297. Sandburg, 387.

298. Johnson, 484–485.

299. Thomas, 446–447.

300. Johnson, 494.

301. Federer, 391.

302. Symonds, 73.

303. Thomas, 402.

304. Thomas, 403.

305. Sandburg, 472–475.

306. Federer, 366.

307. Federer, 366.

308. Federer, 367.

309. Morison, 705–706.

310. Winthrop S. Hudson, *Religion in America* (New York: Charles Scribner's Sons, 1981), 216.

311. Earle E. Cairns, *An Endless Line of Splendor* (Wheaton: Tyndale House Publishers, 1986), 150–151.

312. Sidney E. Ahlstrom, *A Religious History of the American People* (Binghamton: Yale University Press, 1972), 698.

313. Morison, 707.

314. Johnson, 496–497, 501.

315. Johnson, 505–506.

316. Morison, 719.

317. Johnson, 506.

318. Morison, 722–723.

319. Johnson, 507.

320. Morison, 707–708.

321. Johnson, 514–516.

322. Johnson, 517–518.

323. Johnson, 518–521.

324. Johnson, 524–528.

325. Johnson, 513–514.

326. Johnson, 531–533, 544–559.

327. Johnson, 569.

328. Johnson, 573–574.

329. Johnson, 573–574.

330. Johnson, 578.

331. Abram Leon Sachar, *A History of the Jews* (New York: Alfred A Knopf, 1965), 306–307.

332. Sachar, 302.

333. Sachar, 307.

334. Johnson, 578.

335. Johnson, 578.

336. Johnson, 578–579.

337. Federer, 204.

338. Federer, 205.

339. Vinson Synan, *The Holiness-Pentecostal Tradition* (Grand Rapids: William B. Eerdmans Publishing Co., 1997), 29.

340. Synan, 31.

341. Synan, 43.

342. Federer, p. 28.

343. Marshall and Manuel, *The Light*, 145.

344. Marshall and Manuel, *The Light*, 146.

345. Simon Schama, *Citizens, A Chronicle of the French Revolution* (New Yourk: Vintage Books, 1989), 783. (This award-winning book details the French Revolution. A section of the book entitled "Terror is the Order of the Day" describes the mass execution of thousands of French citizens on the guillotines.)

Index

Biographies

BILL HUNTER

B ill Hunter was born in Hereford, Texas, and attended West Texas State University in Canyon, Texas, before studying law at Tulane Law School in New Orleans. For more than 43 years, he has engaged in a small town law practice in Dalhart, Texas, where he lives with his wife, Jeanette. Their grown children are Paula Butler, Janet Tolbert, and Michael Hunter.

Following his law school days, Hunter began an extensive private study of history, Christianity, and the Bible. A spiritual encounter in 1970 and a defining moment at Williamsburg, Virginia, led to the unfolding of a special God-ordained plan for America, which is the subject of this writing.

Hunter's e-mail address is hunters3@xit.net. Visit his Web site at www.billhunter.org.

Charles Timothy Prutzer

C harles Timothy Prutzer was the protégé of Donald Leo Malick and trained under William H. Traher and George Carlson.

His art has been shown in museums and exhibitions around the world, including the Beijing Natural History Museum in the Peoples Republic of China, the Leigh Yawkey Woodson Art Museum in Wausau, Wisconsin, the American Museum of Natural History in New York City, the Burrell Collection in Glasgow, Scotland, and the Museo Nacional de Ciencias Naturales in Madrid, Spain.

Prutzer's illustrations include work for the National Wildlife Federation, Wildlife Stamp Program, and the *Reader's Digest Book of North American Birds.*